Turnin FEAR into POWER

This book is dedicated to the instructors who, with steadfast commitment, put their hearts and bodies on the line to help transform the lives of others. It is especially dedicated to the courageous souls who have faced their biggest demons by walking through the doors to our classes and found the fire of life burning inside. They have always had it; they just needed a little help to remember.

I would also like to give special thanks to my editor, Karen Petersen, who worked tirelessly to compile my seven years of notes, journals, and various ramblings into a cohesive manuscript, the likes of which has never been written before. Karen went the extra mile by participating in FAST Defense classes to be able to bring insight into the program directly to you.

And finally I must give thanks to you, the reader, for having the will and desire to break out of the "box" of self-defense as it has been known for so long and to explore the new horizons that this system affords. May this book be a bright light in a world of ever-growing darkness.

Turning FEAR into POWER

How to Prevail in Verbal Confrontations and against Physical Assaults

Bill Kipp

Paladin Press • Boulder, Colorado

Turning Fear into Power: How to Prevail in Verbal Confrontations and against Physical Assaults
by Bill Kipp

Copyright © 2005 by Bill Kipp

ISBN 13: 978-1-58160-488-7
Printed in the United States of America

Published by Paladin Press, a division of
Paladin Enterprises, Inc.
Gunbarrel Tech Center
7077 Winchester Circle
Boulder, Colorado 80301 USA
+1.303.443.7250

Direct inquiries and/or orders to the above address.

PALADIN, PALADIN PRESS, and the "horse head" design are trademarks belonging to Paladin Enterprises and registered in United States Patent and Trademark Office.

All rights reserved. Except for use in a review, no portion of this book may be reproduced in any form without the express written permission of the publisher.

Neither the author nor the publisher assumes any responsibility for the use or misuse of information contained in this book.

Visit our Web site at www.paladin-press.com

Table of Contents

Preface

I am an expert on fear. I became an expert through years of abuse that was much more damaging emotionally and mentally than physically, though it did occur on a physical level. The end result of any level of abuse is fear.

Although I was not aware of it at the time, these abusive incidents sent me on a long and futile quest to eradicate the evil villain fear from my life. This voyage led me to the martial arts, the U.S. Marine Corps Recon Special Forces; work as a bodyguard, barroom bouncer, and stuntman; years of psychotherapy; and more martial arts. Although these experiences strengthened my resolve to fight the ever-present fear, none were successful in removing it from my life. The problem was that I never received any real training on how to deal with this powerful biochemical and emotional force. Somehow I always managed to dance around the subject of fear rather than tackle it head-on. For a long time I didn't realize that fear is an important instinctual reaction to stressful situations.

And so I fought against it rather than accepting its inevitability and then using my other resources to find a skillful resolution to the underlying problem.

Finally, I stumbled across a self-defense technology that taught people how to deal with their fears effectively and, if necessary, even to use them as incredible sources of power. Propelled by powerful unseen forces, I found myself committing to the long process required to become an instructor of this unique methodology, known generically as scenario-based adrenal stress response training. At the time I had no idea how dramatically it would change my life, even though I saw firsthand how it changed the lives of the students I taught. Although this was "just" a self-defense course, graduates reported experiencing amazing transformations in all facets of their lives. Students who had been abused were literally reclaiming years lost as a result of their abuse. And students with no discernible history of abuse experienced unexpected surges of self-confidence and freedom from the myriad fears that imprison so many of us on a daily basis.

Eventually, I began to see changes in my own life. My fears diminished, and my self-esteem grew stronger. Not only did my fear of physical conflict begin to melt away, but relationships with my family, friends, and coworkers opened up like never before. Perhaps of even greater importance, the smaller, day-to-day fears that really impeded my happiness became much easier to master. Finally, I was no longer controlled by fear.

Seventeen years later this all seems like ancient history. Yet the continual influx of new students serves as a constant reminder of the power fear has over us and the limitless joy that is possible when we learn how to harness and master this powerful force in our lives. In fields as diverse as medicine, warfare, and self-help there has been a great deal of work in recent years addressing the subject of fear and the myriad ways it affects our lives. Yet no work to my knowledge cuts to the source of the problem like scenario-based adrenal stress response training does.

As a self-defense instructor, I have journeyed to the depths of hell and back with my students. Many of these students are survivors of gang rape, ritual abuse, and countless other heartless acts that members of our species inflict upon one another. These people know all too well the insidious effects of intense fear. Prisoners of old abuses that perpetually run through their minds, they are also true survival experts, honing their skills in response to a hypervigilance fueled by the terror that their tormentors might someday return. Often they come to my courses for the next step in their recovery from post-traumatic stress disorder (PTSD) through the referral of a therapist or psychoanalyst. Most of my students have not endured such horrendous acts of violence. Yet they too are limited by the many fears that plague people every day. Invariably, all have felt fear tighten its grip on their minds at some point—fear that dictates their behavior far more than they would like to believe.

Everyone feels fear. But unfortunately, most people have received precious little guidance in how to handle it. On the contrary, I would go so far as to say that society often teaches us how *not* to handle fear. As a result most people respond with a wide range of ineffective behaviors when fear inevitably raises its head—behaviors that diminish their ability to deal with the very thing that caused the fear in the first place!

This book works in two ways. The first is to help identify the obvious and subtle ways that we allow fear to control our lives. Instead of accepting fear as an inevitable and even necessary part of life, we tend to fight against it—expending enormous amounts of life energy in the struggle. The second is to learn how to use fear as a powerful ally. Fear serves a vital purpose in helping to ensure our survival as a species. Animals know this and, when they experience fear, simply listen to the body's cues and respond accordingly. But when we "superior" humans feel fear, we second-guess it, deny it, and literally fight it. Many people have died because of these faulty responses to fear. The challenge is to learn to work within the natural adrenalized fear state that exists to help protect us when we encounter threats and even use it as a tremendous source of power when necessary. We have all heard stories of women lifting cars off pinned children, or sailors tossing 500-pound bombs off the burning decks of aircraft carriers. Such incidents offer concrete evidence of how it is possible to fight *with* this powerful force called fear in the most positive way. Using fear, we can run incredibly fast, get incredibly loud, and fight with incredible strength if we are trained correctly to do so. Adrenal stress response training has helped me and thousands of others harness the power of adrenaline and fear.

At the very least, reading this book will change your perspective on fear forever. At best, it will inspire you to seek out the training you need to make fear your ally. Most people will do anything to protect the ones they love but not necessarily to protect themselves. The information provided in this book will empower you to fight like a mama bear protecting its cubs, only you will be the one you are fighting for. And a by-product of that newfound power is a sense of calm assuredness and self-esteem that many people never experience in their entire lives.

Introduction

The History of Modern-Day Adrenal Stress Response Training

In 1988, the same year my son was born, I accepted an opportunity to take part in a wild odyssey that would forever change my life. It began with my training to become a professional mugger. Not the type of mugger who takes to the streets to prey on innocent victims, but one who plays the part of an attacker realistically enough to scare willing participants into a full adrenal rush so they can learn truly effective self-defense.

Once I completed this training, I began teaching people how to use the incredible power of fear and adrenaline to fight for their lives instead of freezing up and allowing fear to control them. Wearing 35 pounds of padded body armor, I took on the roles of the most vile and depraved monsters that live in many people's worst nightmares. The nastier I was, the better I did my work. The better I did my work, the bigger the breakthroughs my students experienced. I did my work well.

The purpose of the intensive 30-hour program I initially taught was to help women to confront and overcome the intense fear and adrenaline rush brought on by a real-life altercation. Many of my students were referred by rape crisis centers, victim advocates, psychologists, therapists, and friends. Approximately half of them took the course for the proactive real-life self-defense training it affords, and the other half took it to therapeutically work through traumatic events that had already occurred in their lives. The common thread among them was that all had reached some internal threshold where finally facing their worst fears was a better alternative than holding on to them.

I did not create this program. Model Mugging, as it was called, had been around for 16 years before I knew it existed. But, having experienced a thing or two about fear in my own life, I was inexorably drawn to this type of training the minute I saw it.

It all started one warm summer day while I was teaching a martial arts class in Boulder, Colorado, where I live. A student told me about a new self-defense course that was holding a live public demonstration of its latest graduating class of 16 women. Brushing aside my initial eye-rolling dismissal, my student described the event further: "The male instructors wear these big suits and let the students kick the crap out of them. It sounds pretty wild!" My curiosity was piqued. I stopped the class early, and off we went as a group to view this spectacle.

I was little prepared for what I was about to witness. As a black belt martial artist, former marine recon special forces team leader, movie stuntman, professional bodyguard, and barroom bouncer, I thought I had a pretty good handle on the self-defense thing. Boy, was I wrong.

INTRODUCTION

Spellbound, I sat and watched a group of freshly trained women fight for themselves better than I had learned to do in all my years of martial arts and military experience. The padded behemoth instructors repeatedly attacked each student like voracious animals on a hunt. Most astounding to me was that their students were wide-eyed and terrified, yet instead of freezing them up, their terror seemed to motivate them to fight even harder. Fear permeated the room, emanating from the student fighting on the mat as well as the others anticipating their turn. "Woofing," a barrage of vile obscenities, verbal abuse, and threats from the heavily padded instructors, preceded each assault. And systematically each student transformed the powerful force of her fear from dreaded freeze response to venomous verbal defense, followed by forceful strikes to the attacker's head, face, groin, and other vulnerable areas. Over and over, down went the attacker, sometimes locked in embrace with the student, but more often not. Each spectacle was over quickly, ending with the student standing victorious over her fallen and beaten would-be mugger.

Former karate world champion Kathy Marlor fights the bulletmen.

As I witnessed these scenarios, flashbacks raced through my mind like an old movie: images of childhood abuse, of two gang attacks and a gang armed robbery, of the college rape of a loved one, and myriad others.

Then it hit me: *fear is not the enemy at all.* These adrenalized women, my amazing new teachers, were using fear as their ultimate power, the great equalizer, to conquer the evils that threatened to take away their freedom, their happiness, their right to live. Instead of succumbing to the paralysis and dread that the biochemical force of fear can induce, they were using the fear that is a natural, instinctual survival response to a threatening situation as their ally. I felt pity for the poor guys in those protective suits as they somehow withstood each pounding blow to their heads and bodies, only to get up again to play it all over for the next wide-eyed student.

My interest was piqued even further when one of the instructors stated that most graduates of the course reported that they rarely ever needed to use the physical skills they had learned. The awareness and verbal skills they had learned in this unique course usually proved more than adequate to dissuade or deter an attacker before situations got violent.

This was a pivotal experience for me. Two decades of martial training did not prepare me for real-life altercations as well as this program trains people. And I knew all too well about assaults. Having survived dozens of fights, two gang attacks, and an armed robbery, I knew how scary these situations were. Yet all my training managed to dance around the taboo subject of fear. After all, I was a martial arts black belt and a special forces marine. I wasn't supposed to feel fear. I learned a vast amount of fancy technique, yet in not one of my altercations was I ever able to employ more than two or three techniques, and those were very simple at that. After a fruitless 20-year quest to vanquish my own fears, I had finally found the real answer: fear cannot and should not be vanquished. And by accepting its inevitability, we can learn how to cope with and even use its powerful emotional and biochemical effects to our advantage when faced with a threat. Having found my new path, I enthusiastically undertook the yearlong training process to become an instructor. It felt like I had finally come home.

MODERN-DAY ADRENAL STRESS RESPONSE TRAINING

Today I am absolutely convinced that there is no better way to learn effective self-defense than through scenario-based training. Law enforcement agencies and other professional organizations that specialize in combat training have begun to recognized this and have made the switch from old-style, static systems to dynamic scenario-based training.

Although many self-defense instructors have jumped on the adrenal stress response bandwagon, it is my experience that only a select few really understand how the technology works. Many believe that the body armor is the key. It is not. Adrenal stress response training has evolved through more than 30 years of rigorous trial and error. The body armor has evolved to support the teaching methods, not vice versa. The real crux of the technology is the teaching methodology. That methodology has been forged by many talented people over three decades, but if any individual can be called the founder of modern-day adrenal stress response training, it is a gentleman by the name of Matt Thomas. It is from the foundation of his work that I and others have continued to refine the technology over the decades.

It all started in 1971, when a female black belt martial artist was brutally assaulted and raped. This woman experienced an all-too-common reaction to the intense fear she experienced during her assault: she froze. She was tackled to the ground from behind, punched in the back of the head several times while she lay on the ground, and then rolled over so that her assailant ended up sitting on her chest. When she did manage to fight back, her attempts were weak and ineffectual, much like in those dreams where you cannot fight or yell while being attacked. Her frail attempts at defense only incensed her perpetrator to greater violence, and he repeatedly punched her in the face until she gave up, crying. That night she joined the ranks of millions of victims of assault.

This incident prompted her fellow black belt martial arts student Matt Thomas to spend many months investigating police reports on violent crimes. His goal was to determine the most important factors to address when teaching real-life self-defense. Why, he wondered, was this strong young woman with many years of experience in the martial arts unable to defend herself? And if *she* could not effectively thwart an attacker, how could any untrained woman ever stand a chance?

Matt's research uncovered two powerful pieces of information:

1) *People respond the way they were trained.* Matt's friend was trained to deliver strikes in the air with great proficiency and control. Never having hit anyone full-force for real (schools with broken-nosed students don't stay in business very long), she reacted to the attack exactly as she was trained to do: she attempted to hit back but pulled her punches, just as her muscle

memory had been conditioned to do in her karate classroom experience. Furthermore, in her karate system, if someone accidentally fell over during a match, the referees would stop the match and have them stand, bow, and start over. She had never been trained to fight from the ground. Most people are not trained to do anything at all. Thus, the most common responses are to freeze like a deer in the headlights or flail ineffectively.

2) *The crazier person usually wins.* Regardless of martial arts training, it's typically the person who can flip the switch and transform all that fear and adrenaline into go-for-it power who prevails. A person can have all the black belt stripes in the world and still be defeated by someone who has no formal training but has the crazy-person mentality.

Working with these two principles, Matt designed a new type of self-defense course that could be taught in a matter of weeks, focusing on a handful of simple gross motor strikes to vulnerable areas on an attacker's body. Donning protective gear for the final session of his six-week, twelve-hour course, Matt discovered that his students still couldn't fight back very well. Realizing that he had failed to accommodate fully for his number-one principle (people respond the way they were trained), Matt retrained the group all over again.

This time he wore the padding (a pillow over his groin, a bulletproof vest, and a foam-padded hockey helmet on his head) for the duration of the course. Four weeks later at the graduation, the first woman up palm-heeled him in the face so that his head flew backward, totally exposing his groin. So she kneed him in the testicles so hard that his head came forward, and she then drove her knee into his head and knocked him unconscious. Upon rejoining the conscious world, Matt knew he was onto something. He also realized he needed much more padding. In the years that followed, Matt sustained more than 120 significant injuries. With each one he added new pieces of padding. The suit has evolved into the most state-of-the-art body armor in existence today.

Despite the protective armor's importance, it is not the crux of the system Matt developed. It is the teaching methodology itself that is the overriding factor in the success of adrenal stress response training. In a 1993 radio interview in Denver, Matt described how he had incorporated teachings from a wealth of sources in creating his new hybrid self-defense system:

> Our thoughts are like living tapestries where multiple threads from different sources are woven together to form multiple patterns. New threads are added and some old threads are removed as time passes so that our tapestries are ever evolving in size, textures, and even the patterns themselves.
>
> As I reflect on my threads of inspiration, validation, and even negative reinforcement for the Model Mugging Self-Defense for Women program I started to create in 1971 and continued developing for 30 years, the source threads were interwoven from a blend of street combat from my orphanage years in Japan and growing up half-Japanese during the '50s in the United States. This is in addition to my current 43 years of formal martial arts training (I've been a white belt 27 times, a black belt 8); the intellectual con-

> cepts from my six years of formal education at Stanford University and Harvard Medical School; and, most importantly, learning more from my students than they probably learned from me.

This integration of a diverse assortment of inspirations and influences had a dynamic impact on the birth of Matt's revolutionary adrenal stress response self-defense system, which he called Model Mugging after the role-modeling of the male instructors who simulated actual attacks. (Matt originally called his program Role Model Rape Prevention, but his students called him the mugger in his suit, since that was less psychologically threatening than calling him the rapist. So he changed the name to Role Model Mugging, eventually shortening it to Model Mugging.) Here, listed chronologically, are the source threads of Matt's tapestry:

Major Burbery, his army ROTC instructor, was in Special Forces with two tours in Vietnam. He taught Matt the principle of "know your enemy" by having him read translations of works by Mao Tse-Tung, Ho Chi Minh, and Che Gueverra.

Dr. Menachem Amir's book *Patterns in Forcible Rape* convinced Matt to learn more about rapists—invaluable information that he applied to his antirape program. Marvin Wolfgang was a professor who introduced Matt to the psychological profiling that was under development at the FBI. That led to Matt's interviewing incarcerated rapists under the pretext of a psychology research project. Knowing their mental and physical patterns of attack enabled him to design effective defenses against them.

In designing his program, Matt also synthesized key principles from military classics, drawing on the strategic concepts of Sun Tzu's *The Art of War* and Karl von Clausewitz' *On War* and the tactical concepts of Miyamoto Musashi's *The Book of Five Rings*. These resources had certain precepts in common that applied to personal defense. All agreed that a fighting system must

- use deception to confuse the enemy
- be simple to learn and execute
- be capable of being launched unexpectedly
- avoid the strong points of the enemy and focus its strongest weapons against his most vulnerable target
- be extremely aggressive with full physical, mental, and emotional commitment
- attack relentlessly until the enemy is thoroughly defeated—and be flexible enough to function effectively even through the confusion or "fog of war"

Realizing that book knowledge without physical reality is ineffectual, Matt looked to "the Gunny," his archetype ROTC master sergeant, for real-world experience in finding different ways to turn eggheads into soldiers. Matt joined the rifle team, the pistol team, and the drill team and went to the ROTC version of SERE (Survival, Evasion, Resistance, Escape) and Ranger training. Through that training he found that the two most critical military skills applicable to self-defense were the will to survive and creative thinking outside of the box.

Matt also looked to the motto of the U.S. Army's Special Forces (Green Berets), "Free the oppressed," and recognized that it could apply to women—victims of discrimination, beatings, rape, and murder throughout history as well as today. If he was to teach them to fight back—short of the best kind of training that takes years to impart—he needed improvised, effective, available tools with techniques that could be learned quickly and become reflexive.

Dan Millman was Matt's beginning gymnastics coach. He coached using positive reinforcement, self-esteem building, and visualization of optimal results, and he saw the acceptance of mistakes as part of the learning process. Furthermore, he taught by inspiration, actually demonstrating the skills his students needed to learn so they would model themselves after his example. More importantly, he demonstrated the mistakes his students made, crashing and burning theatrically to both relieve the tension and to actively show what they were doing wrong so they would know what to change. At the same time, he would gently remind his students that "practice doesn't make perfect; perfect practice makes perfect." Dan had not yet written *Way of the Peaceful Warrior*, but he was living what he was about to write. Dan was Matt's Socrates.

In an honors program in experimental pathology at Stanford Medical School, Matt was mentored by Klaus Bensch, then chairman of the M.D./Ph.D. program, who taught Matt to think and operate like a scientist. His first advice was to always keep your bullshit detector in high gear, especially about old beliefs. The second was to do the research in the libraries to find multiple reliable sources about the validity of new information. Klaus advised and sponsored Matt on his honors paper and master's thesis and gave him the lab space and materials to perform his experiments (on entirely different topics).

Matt's freshman year dorm's resident faculty, Philip Zimbardo, was a world-famous social psychologist who expanded on Leon Festinger's work on cognitive dissonance. Cognitive dissonance occurs when a person has two opposing ideas at the same time, which creates confusion and often inability to deal with either concept.

With Zimbardo's work in mind, Matt observed that most women perceive of themselves as "nice," yet they need to see themselves as fierce to defend themselves effectively. He also recognized that changing a woman's self-perception is much harder than teaching her physical self-defense moves. Applying some of Zimbardo's psychology methods to ease his students' dissonance, Matt sought to change their perception of themselves through behavioral modification.

Overcoming fear in self-defense students was another huge obstacle. To overcome it, Matt modified Albert Bandura's work on role model mastery, which was originally used to overcome fear of flying, snakes, and so on, into methods that helped women overcome their fear of getting raped. Matt was enthralled with Joseph Campbell's classic *The Hero with a Thousand Faces*, a cross-cultural analysis of the myths of heroes, because he felt that each of his students was on her own hero's journey. The heroes of myth are reluctant, ordinary people who are compelled by the horror of peril to themselves or their community to become warriors and conquer the monster. Borrowing from the archetypes of myth, Matt's program transformed Model Mugging students into their own heroes.

Another of Matt's professors was Colin Pittenrigh, the "father of the biological clock," who taught a course on animal communication. When men attack women, they are behaving more like animals than humans, so Matt reasoned that women needed to learn to communicate like animals when facing these predators. The martial arts *kiai* (shout), or war cry, is a human example of animal communication, and Matt expanded upon this concept in designing Model Mugging. Matt trained his students to resolve conflicts as most powerful predators do—deterring further action with a vicious war cry as opposed to the high-pitched squeal of a victim in distress.

Karl Pribram's work on the neurophysiology of learning convinced Matt to use both positive and negative reinforcement to achieve the same goal in Model Mugging.

Ernest Hilgard was a pioneer in learning and motivation before becoming a pioneer in hypnotherapy at Stanford Medical Center when he and his wife, Josephine, developed the Stanford Hypnotic Susceptibility Scale. Matt was privileged to have taken seminars with them and then applied aspects of their work toward pain reduction in cancer patients to his women's self-defense course.

In designing his self-defense system, Matt also applied research demonstrating that emotional triggers can enhance combat in male bonobos (also known as dwarf chimpanzees, the closest primate to humans with 98.8 percent common DNA). Studies have shown that when bonobos watch other bonobos engage in combat, their testosterone levels rise 1,100 percent. When a bonobo is defeated, his testosterone level drops to below normal in seconds. When a bonobo wins, his testosterone level rises to 1,300 percent above normal, which further prepares him to fight additional males who might think he's tired out. Although no studies had been done in female bonobos, Matt hypothesized that emotional triggers would affect his Model Mugging students similarly, and so they did. Role model muggers easily triggered fury responses in female students who were mothers by telling them he was going to rape or kill their children.

Carl Ebnother was an internist and cardiologist at Stanford Medical School who, in the late '60s, was integrating traditional Western medicine with traditional Eastern medicine. From him Matt learned that autosuggestion was almost as effective as traditional hypnosis but much less psychologically intrusive. This became the basis of the meditation Matt gave his Model Mugging students at the end of the first day of training.

When Matt went to Harvard Medical School, he met David Shapiro, one of the founders of biofeedback. Shapiro was also a martial arts enthusiast and was extremely interested in Matt's boyhood orphanage fighting experiences. Matt was fascinated with the ability to record the physiological control of his autonomic nervous system by being hooked up to machines while practicing various meditation techniques to validate Carl Ebnother's work. Outside the laboratory, Matt tested the ability of the body to rapidly learn new, effective skills through biofeedback via the mugger suit.

Model Mugging/IMPACT

Clearly, this brave new technology was the product of a great deal of knowledge from an impressive array of sources. Over the years the course gained momentum and benefited from the additional input of a variety of talented individuals. The program continued to thrive until many of the major U.S. cities had a chapter.

The late '80s saw an internal rift between the various Model Mugging groups,

Matt Thomas, father of modern-day adrenal stress response training.

and some split off to create IMPACT. This was virtually the same training methodology as Model Mugging, only with a different name. IMPACT grew and still has a strong presence on the East and West Coasts, with satellite groups in between. Both IMPACT and Model Mugging are taught by passionate, talented, and highly trained teams of men and women who specialize in working with people who have experienced severe emotional trauma. These programs have strict quality control and offer the finest training available to help survivors of assault recover and take back their lives.

In 1990 I struck out on my own and created Model Mugging of Colorado. Up to that point, most of the students were women. The fear from some parts of the feminist community was that if we trained male students, we would be creating the next generation of "super muggers." Such thinking showed a real lack of understanding of how this technology works. Disempowered people victimize others. Since this is a technology of empowerment, I theorized that male students would come out of the courses with more sensitivity and compassion. Working directly with Matt, I developed the first Model Mugging for Men program in the country. (I should note that one or two forward-thinking Model Mugging chapters had run some prototype men's programs before this.) A year later the local women's Model Mugging chapter imploded due to internal conflict, and my program expanded to teaching women as well. With an incredible staff of instructors, we trained many thousands of people in the Denver/Boulder area.

RMCAT

In 1992 Peyton Quinn (*Bouncer's Guide to Barroom Brawling*, Paladin Press, 1990) approached me to assist him in his newly created Rocky Mountain Combat

Applications Training (RMCAT) course. Peyton and RMCAT cofounder Mike Haynack had put together this program with the concept of letting go of fancy martial arts technique and teaching only techniques that one of them had used at least three times in real-life situations. The first RMCAT was a five-day workshop where they set up a fake bar and other props to play out highly realistic fight scenarios. Attending this premier RMCAT was a man named Mark Morris, who had brought along the body armor he originally created for Model Mugging. At one point in the course, Mark suited up and let Peyton and Mike fight against him. The two were immediately sold on Mark's protective suit (as is virtually everyone who ever tests it). Following the training, Mike went to Boston to be trained in the body armor so he and Peyton could include it in the next RMCAT. Unfortunately, Mike's father died just before that next class was set to begin, and he was unable to attend.

With just days before a group of students was set to arrive, Peyton was in quite a bind. Since I lived in the area and was already running my own programs, Peyton asked me to help out. I agreed and showed up at the Colorado mountain facility Peyton had rented for the course. Donning my 35 pounds of armor, I fought each of the 17 participants to test the skills Peyton had taught them over the previous two days. The fights were wild and intense, just like in real life. Afterward, the students unanimously rated the instruction as the best they had ever encountered. Someone mentioned that the helmet looked like a silver bullet, and the name "bulletman" was adopted and has stuck ever since.

Over the years I joined forces with several of the world's most experienced bulletmen to teach other RMCATs around the country, each time experimenting with various techniques. We had a great time with this new chance to break out of the martial arts "box," and the fights got so intense that they strained the safety limits of our skill and body armor. But RMCAT became a situation of "too many cooks in the kitchen," and each course was different from the next. We weren't systematically learning what was working and what was not as well as we could have using a more structured regimen. When Peyton created his beautiful RMCAT facility in the mountains of Colorado, he asked me to design a set curriculum and train the instructor team. I designed the basics program and the combat weapons defense modules that are still taught at RMCAT today.

I credit Peyton with helping to keep scenario-based adrenal response training alive. Although he has never been in the bulletman suit, his understanding of this

Author (right) with master bulletman Tim Stott, taking a break at RMCAT.

methodology is well conveyed in his books and videos. Through RMCAT, Peyton created a venue where bullet-men (or muggers, in the Model Mugging vernacular) could work together and play with new ideas and concepts in a light and fun environment. The Model Mugging/IMPACT world was emotionally intense and rife with internal conflict, and we bulletmen had gotten burned out. Personally, I was revitalized by working RMCAT courses, even though they were, and still are, physically arduous.

FAST Defense

I have spent the past 17 years focusing on perfecting and refining the technology of scenario-based adrenal

Full-contact elbow to the head.

stress response training to meet the specific needs of adults, teenagers, children, small businesses, and corporations. These various courses eventually evolved into my FAST (Fear Adrenal Stress Training) Defense system. I continue to run my programs in Colorado, and I also travel extensively, training instructors in both FAST Defense and the EZ Defense program I designed for NAPMA (National Association of Professional Martial Artists). It is with great pride that I can report that I have now trained more instructors than anyone ever has, and these fine people have gone on to teach FAST Defense to a vast multitude of students around the world.

In the process, I have woofed and fought in well over 35,000 scenarios for people of all ages, and I am continuously seek ways to refine the methodology. In FAST Defense, what used to take more than 30 hours can now be accomplished in a single day or less. I have used this shorter format very effectively in the private and corporate sector, training groups from Lucent Technology, MCI, Lockheed Martin, Coors, and many others. The FAST Defense course repertoire includes Basics, Ground Fighting, Defense against Armed Attackers, Defense against Multiple Attackers, Defensive Stick Fighting, Defensive Knife Fighting, and Defensive Shooting.

Last, but certainly not least, is the FAST C.A.T.S. (Child Assertiveness Training Series) program that teaches children ages 6 to 12 how to deal with bullies, molesters, and abductors. Numerous FAST C.A.T.S. graduates have put a stop to their torment from bullies. I also have documented stories of our child graduates using their skills to thwart real-life abductions. Here is one such chilling yet heartwarming testimonial from a father whose son took our FAST C.A.T.S. Basics course:

> Last week our family experienced a near tragedy that you may have heard about. Our son Dakota was approached by a couple of strangers in a car enticing him to take some candy. This happened very close to our house, which made the experience that much more frightening. My son handled the situation in a nearly perfect fashion. He found himself only feet away from two people he did not know, along a sidewalk with a wall, the car door open and feeling pretty uncomfortable. He maintained eye contact, never turned his back to them, did not engage their conversation, cleared himself from the car, and returned straight home safely. He was able to describe the car, the two individuals, and what they were wearing. I truly believe that at that moment in time Dakota utilized all that he has learned and, perhaps without knowing it, projected a sense of confidence and assurance that he was not going to be a victim. I believe that this led to the decision by his predators that trying to take this kid was simply not going to be worth the trouble. I know you taught this exact concept in FAST C.A.T.S., and it is very possible that my son is sleeping in his bed, in his house, this very evening as a result of what you have taught him.
>
> —Kenneth Dickerson, San Diego, California

What price can you possibly put on such a success story? And this is just one of hundreds we receive from the children and adult graduates of FAST Defense.

A FAST C.A.T.S. course graduate employing an antiabduction technique.

Chapter 1

Golden Moments: Preincident Factors

Many self-defense courses stress things like mastering 1,001 special techniques or developing superhuman speed and power to overcome a would-be assassin. Others cash in on the myth that it's necessary to be in fantastic physical shape in order to have any chance of self-defense. The absolute truth is that most fights are won or lost before the first strike is ever thrown. There is a fine art to reading the early signs of an impending altercation and diffusing it before things get violent. I call such moments the "golden moments" because the person who can remain calm and present during these often-intense prefight windows of opportunity can almost always prevent the situation from escalating to physical violence. Better yet, a skilled defender can use these pivotal junctures to take control of the situation and even make it work in his or her favor.

The general public has long been duped into paying huge dollars for health club memberships, martial arts training, kickboxing courses, and a whole new generation of sexy, exotic fighting systems in an effort to gain control of their fear of being attacked. But sadly, precious few of these address the crucial golden moments that can keep almost any altercation from becoming physical.

Golden moments are simply moments in time when we make choices that dictate whether a given situation turns one way or another. They occur when driving, talking to a child or coworker, meeting a strange dog, negotiating a contract, dealing with a panhandler, and virtually any interaction we have. Although golden moments can be subtle and challenging to deal with in the heat of the moment, it certainly doesn't require a doctorate in quantum physics to recognize and capitalize on them. In fact, many people handle the golden moments quite well with little or no conscious effort in various facets of their lives. My wife, Debra, just had an encounter the other day with a rattlesnake that reared up in front of her on a jogging trail. In that encounter there were several golden moments that allowed her to avoid being bitten by this poisonous snake and even remove it from the trail so the next runner wouldn't have to deal with it.

In life we often experience confrontations that, if handled incorrectly, have the potential to escalate to dangerous situations. The more awareness and presence of mind we can have in these golden moments, the better our odds of keeping most situations from becoming dangerous. As you will see, the key is developing an awareness of the multitude of choices that exist in such situations that many of us fail to ever notice.

DOG BITE

To get a good understanding of this concept, let's use

the example of coming across a dog that is tied up outside of a grocery store waiting for its owner. The first golden moment that presents itself involves the choice of whether to walk on by the dog or to stop and pet it. There are a number of factors to consider before making the decision. If you don't like dogs, then it's a no-brainer to simply walk on by. But even the biggest dog lover will take an unconscious mental and visual inventory before petting the pooch: What type of dog is it? What body language is it exhibiting? Is it making eye contact? Is its tail wagging? What condition is the dog in? If Fido doesn't pass the inventory, most people will pass on by. If he does, new golden moments present themselves, and along with them a new set of choices: How should you approach? Do you come in high over the dog and try to pet it on top of the head (a common mistake people make, causing many a dog to look up and snap at the sudden intrusion)? Or do you get down low before approaching and offer the back of your hand for the dog to sniff before you pet him? Again, factored into these choices are the answers to certain questions: What is the dog's response as you approach? Does it welcome you with tail wagging or withdraw suspiciously?

As you can see, there is a great deal of communication that takes place in even a simple interaction such as this one. Essentially, this communication boils down to a series of golden moments. The more aware you are of the subtle messages both parties are conveying, the better chance you have of handling the situation skillfully.

Because it's easy to see the golden moments that occur all the time in our interactions with animals (or their interaction with each other), animal communication is quite valuable to understanding this concept as it applies to humans. Although humans are more sophisticated, much of our communication is very similar to that of our animal friends, especially when we are under duress.

The dog encounter is a simple scenario that is relatively devoid of two factors that can really complicate matters: adrenaline and fear. Unless a dog has bitten you in the past, chances are you won't get too adrenalized by the scenario just described. And if you *have* had a negative incident with a dog, you would probably just walk on by anyway. Ironically, though, the manner of a person who is trying to avoid a dog usually conveys fear and is actually more likely to draw the dog's attention and even aggression.

ROAD RAGE

Road rage is another common situation that is rife with golden moments, and in this scenario fear and adrenaline quickly enter into the picture. It typically begins with a relatively minor traffic-related offense committed by one of two drivers, but sadly it can and often does turn very volatile and even deadly. Golden moments abound in such a situation, but many people get themselves into trouble because they respond to a perceived offense with a knee-jerk reaction that escalates into rage very quickly. Here is how such a situation typically plays out:

You are driving down a highway, and you notice that a car is tailgating very closely. This irritates you. The passing lane is open, and the person could easily pass on by, but for some reason this guy is staying right on your tail.

Golden Moment 1: You take a deep breath and choose not to let it get to you, giving the person the benefit of the doubt by surmising that perhaps he or she is unaware of the tailgating.

This leads to *Golden Moment 2a:* either you both continue driving, or, if you feel your safety is at risk, you put on your right blinker and pull over to allow the tailgater to get around you.

Or it leads to *Golden Moment 2b:* you start imagining what the person might be thinking and take the tailgating as a personal affront to your being, which raises your anger, respiration, and heartbeat to the point where adrenaline starts flowing.

This leads to *Golden Moment 3a:* All is not lost yet. You could realize that you are getting triggered, take some deep breaths, and try to calm down.

Or it leads to *Golden Moment 3b:* You get really pissed off and decide to do a small brake job on "the jerk" to teach him a lesson.

Let's say you opt for the latter. Upon seeing your brake lights suddenly flash, the driver does a panic stop at 60 miles an hour, screeching brakes and burning rubber. If he wasn't ticked off before, he surely is now. With adrenaline surging, he pulls up next to you, middle finger extended and obvious vulgar expletives pouring out of his mouth. This presents you with a couple of possibilities.

Golden Moment 4a: You realize that you perhaps didn't act with the greatest restraint in giving the brake job, take some big breaths, and decide not to engage, ignoring the gesture. You offer a conciliatory wave and avoid spinning out in an emotional burst that would further escalate the situation. Most often such a reaction is enough to de-escalate things.

Golden Moment 4b: You allow your adrenaline and anger to spin out of control, and you fly into a rage. Perhaps you wave your middle finger back at him in a futile attempt to even the playing field. Maybe some colorful obscenities begin spewing from your own lips as you careen down the road, risking life and limb to prove some point, which in your crazed state you can't even identify. You have the vague realization that you may be screwing up, badly. Yet you are so incensed that you couldn't reel yourself in even if you wanted to.

At this point the situation is highly precarious. The only way for it to come to a nonviolent resolution is for one or the other of you to lose face and give in by acknowledging his ridiculous behavior and backing off (*Golden Moment 5a,* which would have been much easier if it had been done in the first place). Or no one gives in (*Golden Moment 5b*), and the situation ends in a fight or a gunshot, or even a horrible accident, possibly hurting or killing the two of you along with innocent others.

As silly as it may seem, variations on the previous scenario occur much more often than you might think. Why? Because under duress people tend to respond to offenses committed by others (whether perceived or actual) with emotional, knee-jerk reactions instead of rational, conscious behavior. Similar situations play out in a thousand different ways all over the globe every day. The common elements are the same type of emotional knee-jerk reactions to fear-induced stressful situations that the road rage incident illustrates so vividly.

BAR FIGHT

Let's look at another common scenario: a barroom altercation.

You are thirsty and want to go out for a drink. There are two local bars in your area. One is a yuppie joint with 30-something-and-older clientele. It's kind of boring, but it's a nice, predictable environment. The other is a sports bar down the street that typically has a line of motorcycles outside. You just watched a Jean Claude Van Damme movie and are kind of fired up. Do you opt to take it easy and wind down by hitting the yuppie bar? Or do you get a little buzz off the idea of heading into the sports bar to see some local "color"? If you choose the yuppie bar (*Golden Moment 1a*), the story is probably over. You'll go in and have a nice, quiet time and go home without incident. But let's say you select door number 2 (*Golden Moment 1b*).

Golden Moment 2a: You walk through the door and enter the bar in a quiet, unassuming manner, surveying the place for a good place to sit, yet not making direct eye contact with anyone.

Golden Moment 2b: You walk in feeling like you need to set an impression that you are "not to be messed with" and inadvertently set yourself up for just the opposite. You strut your stuff, chest puffed out a little more than usual, stern expression on your face, and survey the scene like a hawk looking for lunch, making sure to gaze a little longer at the cute babe at the bar with the black-leather-vested, tattooed biker dude.

Golden Moment 3a: You choose a quiet place in the corner to have a cool one and watch the nearest TV.

Golden Moment 3b: You sidle up to the crowded bar to order a drink and obnoxiously stand in the space where other patrons are trying to walk because you are so damn important and don't intend to take any crap from anyone.

Suddenly, leather-vested tattoo boy comes along on his way to hit the rest room. Standing in his way, you pretend not to see him just to show how superior you are over him and demonstrate to his chick that she deserves to be with a *real* man like you. Irritated, he tries to get by, maybe giving you a bit more shoulder than is necessary.

Golden Moment 4a: You do the adult thing and offer an apology with a smile, which could de-escalate the scene immediately.

Golden Moment 4b: You continue projecting your "real man" image and give some shoulder back. When he looks at you indignantly, you continue down this road by saying, "What the f_ _ _ are you looking at?"

Golden Moment 5: Of course, he now has to respond to save face—unless he's one of the few who can walk on by and not get hooked.

You can see where this is going. There are really only two ways that this can turn out, and they both stink. One way is that one of you backs down, loses face, and goes away to stew on how to exact revenge. The other is that both of you gear up for the inevitable fight. Incidents like this happen all the time, and they often end up badly. Sometimes very badly.

The good news is that with awareness of the common mistakes people make and some proper training, you can learn to use these golden moments to avoid or deter most dangerous situations before they escalate to physical violence. In fact, with practice you can use the golden moments to command situations and steer them to your advantage in rather amazing ways.

Golden moments present themselves not only in negative situations but in potentially happy and fun ones as well. Think of a first or second date. Golden moments abound that will dictate whether and how the relationship will develop. Other examples might include meeting with a new business partner, purchasing a car from a used-car salesman, or establishing a chore schedule with your child.

If you think about it, most of the vast numbers of self-help, personal growth, and spiritual books and workshops are all about dealing with the golden moments that continually arise in our lives. And this is the crux of scenario-based adrenal response training. It is the technology of 1) identifying the emotional, psychological, and biochemical factors that inhibit an individual's ability to contend with the golden moments in stressful situations, and 2) effectively engaging the brain to capitalize on the fear factor in these critical and potentially life-changing human interactions. Through this powerful process, students develop the means to live life on their own terms, consciously and skillfully. They learn to see the multitude of choices that present themselves in each and every situation and gain the power to act on these choices.

Chapter 2

The Power of Adrenaline

If you are old enough to be reading this book, chances are that at some point in your life you have experienced a serious adrenal stress response, also known as fear. Many of us have experienced a good many of them. I have never met a single "sane" person who does not feel fear in a threatening situation. Even the most spiritually enlightened fall prey to the effects of fear. No amount of meditation or "love for one's enemies" stands up under the true adrenal rush when someone is threatened with serious bodily harm.

The single most important factor in effective self-defense is the ability to deal effectively with the adrenaline and fear that naturally arise in a stressful situation. Yet without proper training this powerful biochemical survival mechanism can be your worst enemy. You will react much like a deer in the headlights. How many stories have you heard of a victim "freezing" into compliance with an attacker's wishes? Sadly, it happens all the time. And incidentally, this phenomenon occurs in men as well as women. Over the past 17 years, many men who have taken our course have reported freezing in intense situations. Literally hundreds of my students, many of whom are advanced-level martial arts instructors, have admitted to experiencing the same thing (major kudos to them for having the courage and honesty to admit it).

SOCIAL HYPNOSIS

Whether good or bad, we all have developed some method of dealing with the adrenal rush. Since we are not consciously aware of this phenomenon and receive little or no formal instruction in dealing with it, we tend to react in whichever way we have managed to learn over the years. Some of these ways may be effective, but many are not. In fact, many of the societal messages we have received over the years have actually taught us how *not* to deal with stress and fear correctly.

Hollywood

Movies are one rich source of misinformation on how threatening situations occur. Some of our most illustrious heroes on the big screen unrealistically portray fearless demeanors in the midst of the most chaotic brawls. Many men buy into this false notion that we are not supposed to be afraid lest we be wimps or less than "real men." This dilemma has caused a great deal of conflict among men when fear inevitably rears its ugly face.

Worse yet, it's caused many deaths when people have refused to back down (because Clint Eastwood or Steven Seagal never did), completely overlooking potential nonviolent solutions to confrontations, which led to their pissing off the wrong person armed with a gun or other weapon. These days, women are being conditioned by characters like Charlie's Angels and other tough gals on the big screen who kick ass and take names in superhero fashion. This isn't to say that women shouldn't be empowered. As a bulletman/mugger, I put my body and brain cells on the line regularly to allow my female students to access the incredible power they have within. But unrealistic media portrayals of "woman power" can be as damaging to women as men's macho male role models are.

The flip side of this social hypnosis occurs through portrayals of victims who give up completely when they actually have numerous choices available for defending themselves. For years the movies have portrayed the classic female victim, screaming with paralyzed helplessness at the first hint of trouble. Although there is a new trend toward empowered women superstars, many older women are still influenced by societal conditioning that says a good woman should be quiet and demure, never making a scene or being a bitch and standing by her man amidst the most abusive behavior he or anyone else may exhibit toward her.

Family Fun—The Gift That Keeps on Giving

Family upbringing is another major factor in how people respond in threatening altercations. Avoidance of conflict is a common theme in many families. Such behavior is often handed down from generation to generation without any conscious awareness of it. This often manifests in passive behavior when conflict does inevitably arise. The other end of the spectrum is dealing with conflict in an aggressive and hostile manner, which is also common. This can both overwhelm and threaten youngsters into being passive, or it can push them into becoming overly aggressive themselves. The way our parents dealt with conflict (or not) strongly affects how we currently deal with it. Bad habits abound in our society, and unfortunately they can be gifts that keep on giving right on down the family line. My grandfather was a great old guy who made history as one of the original barnstormer pilots and a pioneer pilot for United Airlines. But he was physically abusive to his wife, a wonderful woman who took care of him and truly believed that his abuse was just a part of life she had to deal with. This greatly affected my mother, who in turn affected us kids in our own ways. Not that she physically abused us; she was and is a wonderful, loving mother. But the subtle effects of her upbringing still had an impact on us. I have no doubt that this conditioning largely determined my passion for helping others not be victims.

Buddy Knows Best

The advice of friends is another rich source of socio-conditioning from which people receive a lot of potentially harmful information. Peer pressure dictates much of our behavior that can far override common sense and get us into worlds of trouble. Many a nice kid has been coerced into doing something stupid, dangerous, and even cruel by a fellow group of "friends" challenging him to do it. This is also true of girls, although it often is carried out in a different manner. Young women can ostracize another girl out of the caste, a form of cruelty that can go far beyond physical torment. So strong is the desire to "belong" that both sexes will often do anything or behave any way that will get them acceptance into a desired affiliation.

Awareness of this form of social hypnosis, which dictates people's actions far more than most would like to admit, is crucial in avoiding the common knee-jerk reactions to conflict. The self-aware individual is much better able to respond with skill and appropriate behavior in situations where most others react emotionally, often with very bad consequences.

Denial of Fear

In some ways women have a big advantage over men, simply because they are more likely to accept fear and thus not deny it. When I was growing up, most boys and young men were never taught that fear was okay. "Fraidy cat" was one of many terms my generation used to denigrate anyone who was afraid. Today there are many more colorful versions. Movies, well-meaning brothers and fathers, and multiple other sources have reinforced that guys should never feel fear lest something be wrong with them. This wreaks havoc in a young man's mind when fear inevitably arises.

The bottom line is that to react effectively to fear, we must somehow break through the classic knee-jerk response to the massive infusion of adrenaline, endorphins, and blood flooding the neural pathways and circulatory system during stressful situations. We are not born with the ability to do this. Some conditioning must occur that pushes us through the freeze barrier into go-for-it power when we need it. There are various triggers that can create this breakthrough from fear into power, such as when a woman's child is threatened and her protective instinct kicks in. But because there are numerous factors stacked against it, few people ever achieve such a breakthrough. However, once they do, most people cease to be victims of fear forever.

And so we begin our journey by looking at how a breakthrough from fear into power occurs. I'll start with my personal experience.

Growing up, I had an older brother who used to beat me up on a fairly regular basis. Since he was so much bigger and stronger, my only survival strategy was to curl up in a ball and take it. Initially I tried to run, but this only seemed to incense him more. Then I tried outrunning him, which stirred him on to even greater violence. The result of this for me was a conditioned terror of being hit, which subsequently caused me to freeze up whenever someone threatened me at school or play. In fact, just being in the proximity of a hostile confrontation caused my legs to shake and my heart rate to explode. Years of training in martial arts, lettering in football, leading my lacrosse team as its captain, and even toughing out marine boot camp all failed to retrain this response. I managed to survive by looking tough enough to keep people from bugging me. But this was a brittle facade. Each incident I was able to bluff my way through left me shaking with weak knees and a queasy stomach. Finally, an incident occurred that really put me to the test.

BREAKTHROUGH

One day while having a beer with a fellow recon marine, I was blindside suckerpunched in the face by the leader of a group of five other "fellow" marines. Neither my buddy nor I saw these guys approach us. We were in a public eating place on our military base and never imagined something like this could happen. The gang was a group of infantry marines who had a chip on their shoulders about the elite recon unit I was in at the time.

The initial sucker punch landed square on my nose, and the fight was on. My first reaction was one of classic denial and total disbelief. The entire scene took on that eerie, slow-motion quality like a nightmare where you feel like you are fighting in quicksand. I remember being in a clench with one of the guys and thinking I should try to kick him in the groin. It seemed like minutes before my leg responded to the call for action and, ever so slowly, arched up somewhere toward his crotch. Either it never made contact or was off the mark because nothing seemed to change, and meanwhile the foglike flurry of violence swarmed around me.

Time became distorted, and though the event probably lasted about two or three minutes (which is extremely long for most fights), it seemed to go on for hours. At one point I found myself at the outside of the melee with the chance to make a run for it. Unfortunately my opportunity was a result of the assaulting mass swarming around my pal caught in the corner of a concrete building. I suddenly found myself in a classic dilemma. Should I run to safety or dive back into the swarm? The fear intensified a hundredfold and felt like a vise clamping on my head. The last vestiges of peripheral vision disappeared, and for a terrifying moment I looked down a long, dark tunnel at my friend curled up in the corner. A sound like a freight train in my head drowned out all other noise.

In a flash, something transformed my fear into full pissed-off fury, and back into the foray I dove, pulling bodies off my friend. I grabbed the first guy who tried to fight back in a headlock and squeezed. Focusing all my intention on the corner of a nearby brick wall, I began marching my captive's head toward it. Driving forward with enraged desire to smash this prized head into the brick corner, I became vaguely aware of some great resistance trying to hold me back. Apparently seeing that I was hell-bent on bloodying their friend, a few guys had grabbed me to try to slow me down. Still moving relentlessly toward the wall, I felt a beelike stinging sensation on the top of my head. Little did I know one of the lads had jumped on my back and was slamming his knuckles onto the top of my skull. (The only reason I can tell this in such detail is that my friend saw it from his corner and recounted it later.) I simply remember an annoying stinging sensation that fueled my fire and made me even stronger.

To make a long story short, head did meet wall just moments before the military police arrived to break things up. Surprisingly, the only injuries were a lacerated head (not mine!) and my own bloody nose from the initial sucker punch. The MPs hauled us all off to jail but soon released my friend and me. The other group was so drunk and obnoxious that they got locked up and were later prosecuted for assault and intent to harm one of the MPs who had arrived on the scene.

My breakthrough occurred in that magic moment when the paralyzing fear turned to enraged anger. In the fear paralysis state I felt like I was fighting underwater, unable to move quickly or think rationally. But once the fear transformed into anger, the whole ghoulish scene took on a startling clarity, and my strength increased tenfold. The usually debilitating effects of the fear adrenal rush were suddenly my greatest allies. I was lucky in this instance. Despite the gravity of the situation, the events that occurred were quite fortuitous for me. In that flash of a moment, everything changed, as my past conditioning to freeze was supercharged into animal-crazed, go-for-it power. In that one short, terrifying melee, my life changed forever.

Note that the trigger that sparked this transformation was not my desire to save myself but to save my recon buddy trapped in the corner. This trigger is not uncommon; most people (particularly survivors of abuse) will fight to protect someone else before they will fight for themselves. Such was the case with me. I remained in the slow-motion fogginess while *I* was being attacked, and only when I saw *my pal* in serious trouble did I break through the fear and fly into the rage. Even though my buddy was the trigger, in that instance I was reconditioned so that fear would never again control me as it did before. I experienced many more fights in the military and later working as a bodyguard/bouncer in Asia, and I never froze again!

The key to adrenal stress response training is to engineer a similar successful breakthrough for each student in a safe and controlled environment. Through a simple yet ingenious systematic process, we do this with remarkable consistency. In developing this reconditioning process, we have had to look deep into the physiological and psychological effects of adrenaline and stress.

ADRENAL STRESS RESPONSE 101

Without proper training, most people either freeze up completely or flail ineffectually in an assault. Traditional combat, martial art, and self-defense training operate within technique-based paradigms, requiring years of intensive effort to master various complicated techniques for dealing with a wide variety of attacks. Yet time and again, empirical evidence shows that such training does not prepare someone for the biochemical and emotional realities of a real-life encounter.

The first real studies of the effects of stress and fear were done back in the 1930s. These studies examined soldiers' ability or lack of ability to send Morse code while under combat-induced stress and found that the subjects had much more difficulty performing in combat conditions than they did in training mode. The next such research studied the ability of Vietnam fighter pilots to discern and operate buttons and switches under duress. Again, the pilots' performance was hindered when they were under duress. As a result of this study, fighter plane cockpits were actually reconfigured to promote greater eye-hand coordination during combat scenarios.

A great deal of additional research has been done in recent years to corroborate my personal experience of the potentially debilitating effects of adrenaline and fear in real-life self-defense situations. In *Sharpening the Warrior's Edge: The Psychology and Science of Training* (PPCT Research Publications, 1995), Bruce Siddle reported the following physiological and psychological effects:

- *Heart rate:* There is a direct correlation between adrenal stress and increased heart rate.

- *Motor performance:* At 115 beats per minute (bpm), gross motor skills can be enhanced, but most people lose fine motor skills so that things such as finger dexterity, eye-hand coordination, and multitasking become difficult. (Bear in mind that it takes very little stress to elicit a 115-bpm heart rate.) At 145 bpm, complex motor skills break down entirely for most people, precluding fancy-technique combinations of almost any sort.

- *Vision:* At about 175 bpm, pupils dilate and flatten, causing what is commonly referred to as "tunnel vision." At this point, visual tracking becomes difficult (very important when dealing with multiple attackers), and the ability to focus on close objects is impaired. (The latter is very significant if there is a weapon involved, since many victims fail to ever see the weapon that could possibly kill them.)

- *Mental function:* At approximately 175 bpm, memory is impaired. "Critical stress amnesia" is a term used to describe this loss of memory. Tests have shown that after a traumatic event, many people recall approximately 30 percent of what happened in the first 24 hours, 50 percent within 48 hours, and 75 percent or more after 72 to 100 hours.

At 185 to 220 bpm, the freeze response begins, often described as the "deer in the headlights" syndrome. This typically leads to ineffective and irrational behavior and even total inability to scream, move, or yell. It is very difficult to break out of this condition, as it becomes a vicious cycle of hypervigilance leading to higher stress levels, leading back to greater hypervigilance, and so on.

To understand the effects of the adrenal rush, it is helpful to know that under duress it causes blood to rush from the major organs to the muscles to prepare for fight or flight. One of the organs losing blood is the brain. As a result, there is a switch from using the more cognitive part of the brain to the more primitive part. Because of this phenomenon, virtually anyone who encounters an intense life-threatening situation will experience most, if not all, of the above-listed effects.

Research has shown that our brain works on two basic levels, which can be expressed in simple terms as the "high road" and the "low road." The high-road brain houses the intellectual and analytic abilities. This portion handles our major cognitive processes of deliberation, analysis, creative thinking, and the myriad other elaborate brain functions that occur on a daily basis. We make plans, strategize, converse, and carry out most of our daily tasks in the high-road part of the brain. The vast potential of the high road is what separates us from the lower animals lacking the complex brain capacities of humans. The low road is responsible for the survival, or reptilian, brain functions. This much simpler part of the brain quickly takes over when a dangerous threat is perceived and an immediate survival reaction is required, such as the fight-or-flight response. Composed of the limbic system (amygdala, hypothalamus, and thalamus), the low-road brain is crucial for the survival of every species on earth. It is important to understand that this is also the emotional center of the brain, which explains why people often exhibit knee-jerk responses instead of conscious, deliberate action in times of duress.

Not only does the brain shift into survival (fight or flight) mode under these conditions, but the body also follows suit. Otherwise simple tasks such as putting a key into a door lock or finding the trigger on a can of mace and the multitude of fine-motor self-defense techniques go right out the window as the body prepares to either fight or flee.

Add to that any past emotional trauma triggered by this new event, as well as sociological conditioning (e.g., don't be a bitch, don't back down, and so on), and dealing effectively with the current threat presents a real challenge. This explains why traditional self-defense training and other complex protection methodologies often fail and why the techniques and methods of scenario-based adrenal stress response conditioning have proven themselves over and over again.

SCENARIO-BASED ADRENAL STRESS RESPONSE CONDITIONING

Traditional technique-based self-defense systems fail to work precisely because they do not engineer the crucial breakthrough from fear into power that must occur in the adrenal rush of a stressful situation. By contrast, the incredible success of scenario-based adrenal stress response training lies not in the endowment of magical techniques that can be used to dispel an enemy, but rather in a teaching methodology that works almost without fail to transform the adrenal rush into power.

This conditioning process uses live scenarios to play out realistic interactions that elicit various levels of the adrenal stress response. The initial set of scenarios is designed to elicit a very small response, and the students practice communication techniques that use body language and verbal skills. Each time the students run through another set of scenarios, the level of adrenal intensity and technique complexity are amped up a notch. The process ends with each student experiencing a fully adrenalized state and employing simple gross motor physical techniques in his or her defense. At each step in the process, the goal is a 100 percent successful outcome of each scenario for every student. If a student is not successful at any particular stage, he or she has an opportunity to redo the scenario and play it out to a successful outcome. Thus, the program is systematically designed to build on each success to enable students to achieve a remarkable level of self-defense in a very short amount of time through progressively transforming their fear into power.

Although simple in concept, this teaching methodology incorporates a number of innovative teaching tools and techniques in order to engineer the desired breakthrough.

Apply Realism

In my experience, simulation training using live scenarios is the optimal way to train people in self-defense. Our instructor teams are well versed in playing out scenarios that are startlingly real for the students. Each scenario played out by a skilled team accomplishes the desired results for that particular section of the course. A great many of our students admit that they initially came to the class not expecting to get adrenalized. Not one of them has ever left dissatisfied!

Generate an Adrenal Rush

Most of the FAST Defense drills use an unpredictable mock assailant, the woofer, who must both generate the adrenal rush in the student and elicit a successful response. The woofer will mimic any number of different personality types to "interview" or test his victims. Sometimes he uses vulgar or abusive language. There is a specific reason for this, and the woofer is trained to understand this and feel secure that it provides a valuable service to the students. A good FAST Defense woofer can intuit what a student needs at each level of the teaching process and push that student to his or her limits while still allowing for a successful experience. In the most advanced drills, the students practice basic physical techniques applying simple, gross motor skills to defend against the bulletman.

Sometimes these fabricated scenarios kick up some pretty wild experiences. I have had situations occur during and after these staged scenarios that made the hair on the back of my neck stand up. Others have left me in tears. One such example happened when I was working with a young woman I knew quite well. She had become a black belt at 16 and was working to overcome childhood sexual abuse by her stepfather, whom I knew as an acquaintance. The fact that I was so tuned in to her situation enabled me to put a great deal of emotion and feeling into playing her abuser during her customized scenario in class. It became so real that she literally felt herself relive the situation, and this time she defeated him. This was a colossal breakthrough for her. Afterward, with both of us in tears, she recounted with awe actually seeing the face of her stepfather on my bulletman helmet. Her custom scenario literally changed her life as she took back the safety and confidence that were stolen from her many years before. This was one of many such situations that really made me understand the power of this work to heal past abuse, which enabled me to play the woofer/bulletman roles as realistically as I possibly could.

Facilitate Visualization

Watching a technique executed correctly over and over again is a powerful learning tool because it creates a picture that imprints upon our muscle memory. Our students watch each and every scenario while standing in line waiting their turn and process each one as if they were actually doing it. This provides a great deal of experience in a relatively short amount of time. In a typical class of 16 students, each participant will do each scenario once and watch it 15 times. Most will learn more from the repetitive exercise of watching the others than they will during their individual scenarios.

Capitalize on Group Dynamics

Survival/adventure courses such as Outward Bound have used group dynamics for decades to dramatically break through old fears and limitations. Adrenal stress response training uses the same principles to achieve maximum results in minimum training time. Strategic facilitation of group safety allows the students to open up and bond with each other. The synergized energy of the group is actually conditioned into each individual performing the scenario, making the training much more powerful than one-on-one training. Students who have taken the course and have been assaulted afterward fre-

A student fights as the class cheers.

quently recount hearing the cheering of their fellow students as they fought off their attacker(s). The subconscious voices helped kick the adrenal stress conditioning into gear, empowering them to fight even harder.

Train the Brain

Students begin by learning proper awareness skills so that they recognize prefight indicators that will help them avoid getting drawn into a confrontation in the first place. They also gain an awareness of the subtle ways in which potential victims communicate nonverbally with predators. Interviews with convicted felons offer overwhelming evidence that predators look for specific cues from their intended victims. The failure of a potential victim to exhibit these cues is often enough to deter an attack before it ever begins. Thus, FAST Defense students acquire the nonverbal communications skills to present themselves in a manner that is neither passive nor aggressive but, rather, assertive.

Train the Voice

Students must also learn verbal skills to effectively thwart an assault before it becomes physically violent. Perhaps the most important self-defense skill of all, verbal defense is also the most neglected. Studies show that 80 percent of assaults on women are successfully carried out through verbal threat alone, and the vast majority of assaults on men are preceded by verbal provocation. Thus, a good verbal defense is enough to stop most attackers in their tracks.

Teach Appropriate Action

The real trick to effective self-defense is in determining the level of threat and reacting with the appropriate level of response. Most people fail to assess the threat level correctly and either underreact and become victims or overreact and exacerbate the situation. FAST Defense students learn to identify a range of threat levels and then respond appropriately. In the process, the social conditioning that can get both men and women into trouble is deprogrammed and replaced with new, appropriate responses.

Emphasize Breathing

This may seem silly to mention, as certainly everyone knows how to breathe. But breathing is the "antifreeze" secret. Most people hold their breath under duress and quickly lose power and control of their minds and bodies. Holding the breath is often the first symptom in a cascade of failures that can lead to a total freeze-up in the heat of the moment. We emphasize breathing through every step of our training. We do this by having the students vocalize the name of the technique they are applying. Saying the technique helps to anchor it in the students' brains and, more importantly, trains them to breathe, since one must breathe in order to vocalize. In this way, the voice becomes the gateway to power during the fight scenarios, where students can say anything they want to or just yell with spirit. As one student so eloquently stated years ago after a big breakthrough, "I discovered that the way to get the power I have inside to work for me outside is to use my voice!"

Keep It Simple

In adrenal stress response training, we focus on a handful of very simple strikes delivered with full adrenal force. Since fine motor skills tend to go right out the window in the adrenal rush of a real attack, all physical defense techniques must utilize simple gross motor skills if they are to be accessible and applicable when a person is under duress. Most importantly, students of this training find that by not having to think about the techniques, they have greater ability to relax under the adrenal rush and maintain the ideal heart rate for optimum effectiveness (115 to 145 bpm).

* * *

As you can see, self-defense must encompass a wide variety of skills in order to be effective in countering the diverse confrontations and threatening situations that people experience every day. The good news is that modern technology has afforded us the means to impart these skills quickly and relatively inexpensively. Years of martial arts training are not required to learn the simple skills necessary to defend against most attackers. There are now short self-defense courses including all of the above information that enable students to attain amazingly consistent results in just a few hours. From there, students can continue on to advanced-level courses that include ground fighting, weapons defense, knife and firearms training, and even defense against multiple assailants.

One thing is for sure, self-defense is not rocket science, and through scenario-based adrenal stress response training, virtually anyone can learn to take care of him- or herself better and more quickly than was ever before possible. Not only is there a growing need for good self-defense as our society becomes more violent, but these skills also translate to other walks of life where any sort of confrontation occurs. Graduates of our courses report again and again how empowered they feel at work, home, and in virtually every facet of their lives after taking one of our short courses. They learn that the dreaded adrenaline rush can actually become their best friend in the world should they ever need to draw upon it.

Chapter 3

The FAST Difference

An Anthony Robbins seminar I attended in 2002 called "Date with Destiny" presented the idea that for any training to have a lasting effect, you must stimulate or educate the mind, the emotions, and the body. Although this statement was made in the context of personal development and self-improvement, it directly applies to scenario-based adrenal stress response training. In fact, if any type of training fails to address any of these three areas, it will not last and will probably fail in a real situation.

Think of how many times you may have taken a CPR course. Though filled with valuable information, these courses are taught in sterile environments where an instructor lectures and then you practice the material presented on a training dummy. Your mind is trained, as is your body to some extent, but the emotional part of the brain is not involved. How will this serve you when you are on the scene of an accident and someone has gone into cardiac arrest and you are in a full adrenal rush? Now, how many breaths was it to how many heart pumps? This important information is stored in a different part of the brain (the high road) than the part that is functioning under the extreme conditions of a real accident (the low road). If such courses were taught in adrenal stress mode, they would be much more effective!

Think back to a time when you were at a rock concert (or any concert with your favorite band). The music was blasting, and you were singing the words (mind). The whole place was filled with waves of electric energy (emotions), and you were literally dancing in your seat with enthusiasm (body). Years later (decades for some of us), you hear the same song again, and instantly you feel a rush of energy as that euphoric state overwhelms you again.

On a less happy note, do you get an instant adrenaline rush when you see flashing blue lights in the rearview mirror of your car? Think back to the first time you were pulled over. Your mind, emotions, and body (even though you were simply driving) were definitely triggered. And that first time never leaves you. Later on, you see the same lights, and the rush is there in the blink of an eye, whether you were the culprit or not. The police lights exist as an anchor.

Likewise, in the context of teaching self-defense, it is essential to skillfully affect students' minds, emotions, and bodies to produce skills that will last. This is easier to do than most people believe.

In FAST Defense we put our students through scenarios that start at an easy level and work up in intensity and difficulty. In each scenario the entire class lines up along one wall of the classroom. First we instruct the students on exactly what they will be doing in the drill, explaining what the woofer will be doing and what the students will do. This trains the *mind*. Then each student comes out one at a time in and, in front of the entire group, the coach prepares him or her to do the scenario. By design, the very act of being singled out in front of fellow students elicits an adrenal rush (fear, nervousness, performance anxiety). Usually it doesn't take much (or sometimes *any*) verbal stimulation by the woofer to get the adrenaline flowing. This trains the *emotions*. Finally, the student (who is always assisted by a coach) performs the particular action required, as called on by the scenario, and returns to the line. This trains the *body*.

Just as a person who was victimized in a single incident and froze under duress will tend to freeze in subsequent scary situations, the scenarios played out in adrenal stress response training can literally anchor new, positive action modes in students in a very short amount of time by impacting the mind, emotions, and body. Although more of such training is always better, it is conceivable that the student who never takes another class after our initial 3.5-hour FAST Defense course will retain that reconditioned response for many years to come, if not forever!

ASYMMETRIC VS. SYMMETRIC TRAINING

Self-defense has become a hot topic in today's world as stress levels rise and violence increases. In our land of opportunity, various groups have capitalized on the trend toward scenario- or reality-based training, espousing this or that particular form of it. Yet it's been my experience that few of these groups truly understand how scenario-based adrenal stress response training is meant to work. Even though it is not rocket science, it must be taught responsibly and cohesively, or it can do more harm than good. I constantly get reports from folks who have tried teaching various types of live, scenario-based training and have gotten injured. I also receive reports from students who have attended classes that went horribly wrong. Add the current liability issues to the mix, and at the other extreme it's easy to see how scenario-based adrenal stress response training has become diluted in many cases.

Scenario-based training is not a new concept by any means. Warrior cultures as far back as the Spartans of ancient Greece have embraced this model to prepare their soldiers for combat. And today its use is not limited to combat. Scenario-based training is used to train athletes as well as members of debate teams. In fact, the concept is now applied in so many vocations that its application in self-defense has become somewhat distorted in some cases. I believe this is because many instructors lack a clear understanding of the difference between the traditional, *symmetric* technique-based training paradigm that has been used ineffectually for so long and the modern scenario-based training paradigm, which is *asymmetric*.

Quite simply, symmetric training is an event where two or more participants engage in a preassigned athletic contest, adhering to certain rules and regulations intended to keep the event safe and orderly as they compete toward whatever victory or goal they have agreed to. A good example of this is sparring in a martial arts class. Although it may well be a good adrenalizing experience for the participants, it is nevertheless done in a symmetrical fashion: both sides know the rules and agree to abide by them, both sides know this is not a life-or-death struggle, and both sides come to the event psychologically prepared.

Martial arts sparring can certainly become quite spirited and intense. Perhaps the most extreme example of this is the Ultimate Fighting Challenge or the various other mixed martial arts (MMA) and no-holds-barred, full-contact events that exist. There can be no doubt that the participants are extremely fired up and that the stakes often include bodily injury. But still, it is unlike a real fight in that the combatants show up for the event physically well trained (or at least they should) and psychologically prepared to engage in the competition. Boxing matches fall into the same category, as do wrestling, jiu-jitsu, judo, and myriad other sport combat events.

Training for such an event typically consists of performing symmetric exercises to practice various skills, all of which build upon each other in terms of their complexity and the stress levels they produce. Eventually, the combatant achieves a good skill level, confidence, and ability to apply these skills and techniques against a determined opponent. Although the training may be arduous, students are not typically subjected to the level of nervousness and anxiety that they experience in the actual event. Through repetition, they obtain the experience of dealing with this nervousness and eventually become accustomed to it. Still, the most important factor contributing to success in the ring or octagon is the technical ability of one fighter over another. Symmetric training focuses more on technique and less on spirit so that participants can safely engage in an athletic contest to test their technical and physical abilities.

I need to be clear that a well-trained full-contact ring or octagon fighter would probably not be someone you would want to have to fight in the street. Nevertheless, many full-contact fighters have taken FAST Defense courses and noted that adrenal stress response training is a very different experience than fighting in an organized competition. Even the most intense full-contact competition is still based on a symmetric paradigm: both combatants show up psychologically prepared to fight each other, and both adhere to prescribed rules and limitations. By contrast, adrenal stress response training employs various strategies to take each combatant by surprise, even though they know they are about to be attacked. For instance, in FAST Defense we have the students close their eyes so they cannot see the attack coming. In addition, ring fighters who take our course are often quite surprised by the power of our instructors' verbal provocation alone. Remember, real attackers commonly use such verbal attacks to intimidate their victims with great success, yet these are never allowed or addressed in ring competition.

Asymmetric training is similar in some ways to symmetric training. Safety is still an important issue (or should be), and there are usually some predetermined rules as well as prescribed techniques for addressing the particular parameters of each scenario. However, there are some important distinctions. Primary among them is that in asymmetric training, teaching the technique itself is secondary to training the student to apply that technique under duress. When this type of training is done correctly, the technique is learned first in a slow-motion, no-stress environment where the body movement and mechanics are stressed. Rather than focusing on the fine points of technique (which typically go right out the window in real encounters anyway), the instructors focus on teaching the student to deal with the level of intimidation in each scenario and respond in a congruent and effective manner.

Another distinction is that asymmetric adrenal stress response training is predicated on 100 percent success for every student through every scenario. The scenarios are specifically designed to increase the intensity in bite-size, digestible chunks so that students get neither bored nor overwhelmed. Each time a technique is practiced, the stress level is increased incrementally. The instructor team works with each student in a deliberate manner to push him or her as hard as possible while still ensuring a positive outcome every step of the way. If one student is particularly stronger or weaker than another, the woofer simply modifies his woof accordingly, and the coach takes a more active role to fine-tune that student. If the instructors feel that the student would benefit from doing the scenario again, they bring that student right back out and repeat the drill.

A third distinction is that asymmetric training is concept-based rather than technique-based. Many people who are unfamiliar with adrenal stress response training consider it to be strictly physical—that is, the students learn to channel adrenaline into the fight and beat up the padded "dummy." Although this is an important facet of the training, few of our graduates ever have to use their physical skills in real-life encounters because of the awareness and verbal skills they acquired in training. These skills translate to the ability to deal with fear as much or more than physical defense skills do.

The fact that more than 80 percent of assaults on women are successfully carried out with verbal threat alone is a clear indication that the verbal crap, or woof, that an attacker puts out causes most women to freeze up. Men too fall prey to a good woof, getting hooked by verbal provocation more often than not. A verbal threat can be as adrenalizing as a physical threat, if not more so. And because they have never learned to deal with this type of verbal intimidation correctly, many people succumb to fear and choke. Therefore, the scenarios in adrenal stress response training must encompass not only physical drills but verbal as well.

At the training's most extreme levels, a padded attacker fully adrenalizes the student and attacks in an unspecified manner, requiring the student to adapt and respond to the threat while channeling the adrenal fear rush into action and power. This is indeed extreme self-defense, and the padded attacker needs a great deal of skill and safety equipment to survive the onslaught of a fully adrenalized individual. Most students say that their fight scenarios seemed just as real as actual altercations they have experienced in real life. Indeed, these fights look very much like real fights, where fine motor skills are nonexistent and the victor is not necessarily the one with the most skill but rather the one who can flip the switch and go for it with power and conviction.

The fact that asymmetric scenario based training is concept-based rather than technique-based is key to its efficacy. Real-life encounters have shown that the person most able to deal with and apply the adrenal rush through simple gross-motor techniques will respond much more effectively to a threat than someone with incredible physical dexterity (and perhaps multiple stripes on his or her black belt) who has not learned to deal with the adrenal rush. This is not a knock on traditional martial arts; they are a wonderful way to build self-discipline, strength, endurance, and much more. But the martial arts need a bridge to help students apply the symmetrical training learned in the dojo or training hall to the real world, where events happen in a very asymmetrical manner. Adrenal stress response training serves as that bridge.

In short, asymmetric training deals with a much larger set of variables than symmetric training. Likewise, real-life altercations typically involve a complex set of interpersonal human dynamics and unpredictable attacks. Responding to and defending against these effectively requires flexibility and finesse. Asymmetric training, when implemented correctly, equips students with a variety of skills and abilities that enable them to adapt and respond to a wide range of potential threats. This skill set encompasses and goes far beyond that imparted by symmetrical physical technique training.

GROUP DYNAMICS

Very often I get feedback from FAST Defense graduates regarding the amazing level of camaraderie they experienced with fellow classmates during their adrenal stress response training. Female and male students alike report how great it was to feel the incredible group support as they faced internal (and external) demons and broke through preconceived limitations. We consciously use group dynamics to get people to do things they might not be able to do on their own, much like Outward Bound does when tasking a class of students to overcome a wall or ropes course. The experience brings individuals together into a cohesive, dynamic crew working together to attain a common goal.

In the beginning of each course, I make the point that although the classroom is filled with individuals who have come to take a self-defense course, they are forming a team to help each other through the experience. In the opening circle (where we take time to set the stage for the experience), I draw an analogy to sitting around a campfire before setting off on a raft trip:

> The river is flowing slowly behind us, but downriver a bit the rapids begin and will increase

> in size and ferocity throughout the rest of the trip. Shortly, we will enter the boat, and each student will have a paddle. If each individual pitches in and works together, then as a team we will be able to negotiate incredible rapids and even enjoy the ride more. This also means that at any point, if any member of the group needs to put his or her paddle down for any reason at all, then the rest of us must take the opportunity to dig in a little harder to pull for that person instead of tossing him or her out of the boat, as society often does.

In group dynamics this is often termed "creating the safe container" for the group. It enables each person present to feel okay about having the individual experience of facing fears and achieving breakthroughs while working for the collective toward the common goal, which is getting through each rapid. It also brings the staff in as group participants instead of creating a separation between "us" and "them." The staff may be the guides, but we are all in the raft together. Because a high number of students come to our courses to work through past victimizations, we insist on a pact of confidentiality between all participants at the beginning of each course so that whatever personal stories or experiences may come up will stay within the safe confines of the group. (Out of respect for this confidentiality pact, I have changed the names of the participants in each of the real-life stories included in this book.) Safety is very important, particularly for prior victims of sexual and physical abuse who may want to open those old doors and clean house of old victimizations that are still holding them back from living a vital and powerful life.

(When I taught this program in the Denver area, we had psychologists who took the course say it was worth three years of intensive therapy in terms of its ability to really get inside the deeper issues that bound survivors to repetitive fear and helplessness. They would even send us some of their toughest cases to enable them to get that next level of healing. I could write an entire book on the amazing breakthroughs we had with these people and how such events irrevocably transformed their lives—not to mention dramatically touched my own!)

The most powerful use of group dynamics occurs during the physical fights depicting scenarios where awareness and verbal skills have failed and physical defense becomes necessary. The instant the student fights back, the entire line of fellow students is encouraged to chime in and cheer for that student. This works on two levels:

1) The students in the line increase their skill and power exponentially by being visually involved with each fight, compiling and assessing the data of each scenario and problem-solving for the defender as if they were out there themselves. They are also transforming all their nervous energy into action and power. Most students say it's more nerve-wracking waiting their turn in line than doing the actual fights. The line is a great opportunity for each student to repeatedly recondition the freeze-or-flail response into conscious assessment and appropriate response.

2) The student in the actual scenario feeds off the collective power of the line, making him or her fight with even more spirit and power. It's an amazing thing to feel when the whole line is cranked up and really cheering like hell for each other (this is the collective

paddling in the rapid referred to earlier). Inside the bulletman suit, we literally see the defender's eyes fire up, and it's very much like what one might imagine fighting a really pissed-off Bengal tiger must be like. It takes the safety of the suit and intensive training to survive the onslaught of a fully adrenalized person fighting for his or her life.

A common concern that students raise is the fact that in real life there is no line of supporters cheering for the victim to help incite the defender into action. Our response is that after this training there will be! Many students have reported actually hearing the cheering of their classmates in their subconscious mind during real assaults and have told us that it fired them up just as it did in class. This is just one example of this training's ability to "anchor" positive action modes in the low-road brain.

GENDER SEGREGATION VS. INTEGRATION

In the field of scenario-based adrenal stress response training, there has been a great deal of controversy regarding the matter of training women and men separately versus together and who should train whom. Some say that only women should teach women. Others say that men can train women but that the classes should be segregated according to gender. Yet another school of thought says that mixed classes are fine and can be taught by men or women. It is my experience that all of these formats can work, depending on the specific level of emotional work versus physical training that is being taught and the relative skill level of the instructors. But in FAST Defense we embrace the integrated model.

Integrated Classes

When teaching short, basics-level self-defense courses to the general public, I find that integrated classes of both sexes work quite well. The aim of such a class is to educate people to the common mistakes people make that can get them into trouble and how to avoid trouble in the first place. This can be done very effectively with both sexes at the same time. Typically, students are surprised to see that there are more commonalities than differences between men and women in terms of how they deal with fear.

With just a small amount of tweaking, the instructor can modify the individual scenarios to be gender-specific. Otherwise I find that the basic concepts of self-defense apply equally to both sexes, and most students appreciate seeing how the other gender responds in these situations. We all must overcome the debilitating effects of fear and adrenaline to respond effectively to danger. Even though there are differences in how women are attacked versus how men are attacked, the mechanism to overcome the adrenal fear rush is essentially the same for both genders.

Gender-Specific Classes

Programs exist around the United States and abroad that consist of longer courses designed to be very emotionally intense. I owned and taught such a program for more than 12 years, and it was one of the most demanding yet rewarding experiences of my life. My team worked with students ranging from those with no history of abuse or victimization to multiple rape and ritualistic abuse survivors. The transformation of many of our students was no less than stunning. Victims who had lost years or decades of happy, productive lives literally cleaned house of the old abuses and burst forth with a vibrancy that bordered on the miraculous.

These intensive courses worked best when segregated by gender. The students required an extreme level of emotional safety to permit them to open up to the level that was required of them to do such powerful work.

I have found that female-only courses are best led by a strong yet compassionate woman accompanied by equally caring men to assist in instructing and playing the attackers in the scenarios. I believe it is important that the students get to know the male instructors and see them as the caring, empathetic men that they must be to take part in such a program. This important human interaction provides a greater sense of healing for these women, who most likely were victimized by men. Ironically, it also allows the women to fight more intensely once the scenarios begin. Initially seeing that the male instructors are nice guys and truly committed to the empowerment of women enables the female students to feel greater safety in fighting when the guys later play out the roles of the nasty characters in the assault scenarios. This may sound contradictory, since real-life attackers are not "good" guys at all. But this seeming contradiction serves an important purpose.

In my experience, in order for most women to give themselves permission to fight back, they must first overcome a great deal of socialization that tells them to be nice and cooperative—and not be a bitch. In FAST Defense we focus on the lofty goal of creating a new social order, and the first step toward attaining that goal is to create a sense of safety for the women that enables them to open up and break out of their shells. The better we are at creating this safety net at the outset, the easier it is for the women to smash through the old conditioning that keeps so many of them locked in victim mentality. Personal experience shows that women typically respond favorably to male instructors, as do men to female instructors. Female students have had extraordinary breakthroughs when working through past abuses by men with our male instructors. Julie is one such student.

The Story of Julie

As already stated, many of our students come to us because of prior abuse. Sometimes they talk about their histories right away in class, and sometimes it takes a good deal longer, if they ever open up at all.

By chance, a woman named Julie who attended one of our weekend intensive courses many years ago ended up sitting next to me in the opening circle where we introduce the staff and allow the students to introduce themselves. As I spoke about the history of our training, Julie subtly kept inching farther and farther away from me. By the end of my five-minute talk she had literally moved from a distance of about a foot away to a good yard. She probably would have gone farther, but she had come up against the student sitting next to her on the other side.

Having become quite sensitive to the energy I put out and the energy of our students, I was painfully aware of the discomfort this poor woman was feeling. Knowing that each student was about to get the chance to introduce herself, I simply relaxed into the situation to see what Julie would have to say on her turn, hoping she would shed some light on what was frightening her. By the time it was Julie's turn to speak, she was visibly shaking from nervousness. To her immense credit, she admitted that it was very difficult for her to be there because of childhood abuse she had suffered, and that just sitting next to a man was enough to almost completely unnerve her.

As she spoke, the words started to come faster. A heart-wrenching story poured forth as she recounted seeing her best friend beaten to death by a neighborhood man whom she knew. The two of them were playing in a bedroom, and Julie somehow managed to survive by crawling under a bed to hide just a few feet away from the horrible incident. At the time she was 5 years old. This led her to retreat deep within the inner walls of her psyche, where she still lived much of the time. Growing up in this withdrawn state had made her an attractive choice for other predators in her life, and various victimizations marked her rise to womanhood, leaving some scars visible but many more unseen.

Julie gained weight, both as a defensive mechanism to deter potential predators and as a protective layer to hide behind. After years of therapy, she eventually married a wonderful guy and had three beautiful children. But a huge part of her always remained hidden far away, never finding the security she needed to show that precious 5-year-old girl trapped inside her all the joy that the world has to offer.

Julie was one of many of our students who showed me what courage really is. Despite her horrific past, she hung in there through that long weekend with the tenacity of a warrior prepared to fight to the death. Something had snapped inside that pushed her over the threshold to finally face the fears that had ruled her life for so long—fears that most of us could never begin to fathom. She had found the courage to fight for herself, becoming both the mama-bear protector and the innocent, vulnerable cub. I will never forget the moment she broke through the victimization and grief, discovering the exhilaration of realizing she really was a beautiful person worth fighting for. In that moment Julie experienced an amazing metamorphosis that transformed her and everyone around her. At the end of class, Julie gave me a hug and thanked me for helping her take back her life.

To my great pleasure, Julie kept in close touch with us for years after her class, returning to take every advanced course we offered. Her husband came and took our men's course. Years later, I even had the pleasure of working with her children in one of our first courses for kids. They all candidly conveyed the healing that had taken place and continued to occur within their family.

Never in all my years of martial arts and marine corps special forces training did I come across anyone with the courage, spirit, and heart that Julie showed that weekend. The true meaning of human spirit was revealed to us all through her will to survive and be free. For me it was (and still is) humbling to share in the process of a woman finding her power. Her story is one of hundreds I have experienced in my career as an instructor. Whenever I hear separatist instructors say that only women should teach women, I think of Julie and the gifts we all received from her strength and willingness to show up and stay in that class.

Success stories like Julie's have been the motivating force compelling me to continue doing this work year after year.

Chapter 4

Developing Awareness

By now you should be getting the idea that self-defense goes far beyond mere physical technique. Yet most self-defense courses devote a great deal if not all of their focus to physical techniques meant to deter an attacker. Unfortunately, arming students with only physical skills leaves out huge pieces of information that are crucial in effectively stopping a fight before it occurs. Add to that the fact that much of the physical skills training taught is relatively ineffectual in a real encounter, and the harsh truth is that most self-defense training can actually set students up for failure, sometimes with catastrophic results.

Comprehensive self-defense should begin with teaching a variety of awareness skills to help the student deal with a potential confrontation and prevent it from becoming violent. Although there are random attacks (such as my marine gang attack) where little or no warning signs are given, these represent a very small percentage of real-life confrontations. And in truth, even most random attacks provide some sort of warning signal if you are acutely aware of your surroundings at all times. In the case of the gang attack that occurred on our marine base, my buddy and I were lulled into a false sense of security because we were on our own base and never conceived that such an incident would occur there. Because of this, we failed to exercise proper situational awareness. The harsh truth is, attacks can happen anywhere and any time.

Almost every threatening situation presents any number of opportunities for avoidance, de-escalation, or deterrence if the intended victim knows what to look for and has tools to respond correctly. Good awareness skills alone work surprisingly often in preventing violence.

Awareness falls into two distinct categories: *external awareness* (what is happening outside of our bodies) and *internal awareness* (what is happening inside our bodies).

EXTERNAL AWARENESS

Most typical self-defense courses will cover rudimentary external awareness—things like, "Don't walk down a dark alley in the middle of the night." Although awareness of your surroundings is important, there is much more to it than that. External awareness has many facets, ranging from your environment and who is around you to the time of day it is to possible safe versus unsafe places in the area to the body cues of a potential threat to a wide variety of situational awareness skills that can tip you off to potential danger before it ever begins.

For children, external awareness also entails knowing personal identification information, never going anywhere with a stranger, what to do when lost, what to do when at home alone, safe touch versus inappropriate touch, and so on.

The more aware you are of your surroundings, the people around you, and the environment you are in, the better chance you have of detecting a possible threat. In most situations the potential attacker gives a number of clues that can tip off the wary victim to danger. There is an absolute correlation between early detection and successful reaction. Just as it's much easier to stop a car moving at 5 miles per hour than one going 40, so it is with a violent encounter.

In scenario-based adrenal stress training, we take external awareness a step further by educating students on the typical bully or predator's mind-set. A great deal of research has been done on what an attacker looks for when he (or she) picks a potential victim. (Although statistically most predators are male, incidents of violence between females are growing rapidly!) The consensus is that bullies and almost all predators are looking for easy victims. Providing our students with awareness skills for understanding and reading what is happening inside the mind of a typical predator greatly helps demystify the predator—often imagined as the evil monster portrayed in movies. So many children and adults feel they have no chance of surviving against a bully or predator, and this simply isn't so. It's just that no one ever gave them the means to do it effectively. By developing awareness of what predators look for, you can stop many assaults before they ever occur by not presenting yourself as easy prey to the predators of the world.

INTERNAL AWARENESS

What most self-defense courses fail to address is *internal awareness* of the various biochemical, intellectual, and emotional responses we experience in times of duress that can keep us from taking action at all or cause us to act ineffectively, such as by flailing or freezing, when we do respond. If we aren't aware of them, we can't harness these powerful forces of nature to work for us instead of against us, and all the fancy martial arts technique or intellectual power in the world won't help a bit.

Case in point: A marine corps buddy of mine was trained from early childhood in the martial arts by his somewhat famous martial arts father who ran a karate school. There was no doubt about my fellow marine's highly tuned martial abilities when our recon teams trained and sparred together. Yet he took so many real-life beatings as we traveled throughout Asia that he became the running joke of our unit. He would continually get himself into these ridiculous situations where his safety was compromised before he ever had the chance to use his great physical prowess. Once he had to jump out of a third-story window to avoid being knifed by a group of locals during a card game in a Filipino barrio.

Now, one could rightfully question my buddy's intellectual capacity, which allowed him to get into so many predicaments. We sure did! But my point is that his martial arts training failed him on two major levels:

1) He refused to listen to his own inner voices of common sense and wisdom. His conditioning while growing up was to use his reputation and machismo to power through any situation that came up in his somewhat sheltered existence. When he suddenly found himself in a much more complicated and dangerous world than he was raised in, his conditioned denial and macho bravado became real liabilities as they overrode his common sense.

2) His ultimate backup system of his martial arts ability didn't work for him. In the times he attempted to fight with his great, complicated techniques, most often they failed him. Why? All of his earlier training occurred in the controlled environment of a karate school where he never experienced the intense fear and adrenaline that occurs in these real-life experiences. Not only was he unaware of what was happening to him internally in the heat of a real altercation, but he had no idea how to use it to his advantage.

The Color Code of Awareness

Self-defense is as simple as making the appropriate response to a given threat—neither underreacting and becoming a victim nor overreacting and exacerbating the problem. Without training, however, it can be difficult to assess the level of threat and thus respond effectively. The color code of awareness has been used in many contexts, including military and law enforcement, to provide a simple frame of reference for identifying the level of threat in order to determine the corresponding appropriate level of defensive action. It also works well in the context of civilian self-defense. The variation of the color code that we use in FAST Defense represents three basic levels of human interaction that lead up to but do not include physical force. They consist of yellow alert (normal conversation, low-level threat), orange alert (moderately intense threat), and red alert (very intense threat, on the verge of physical violence). Bear in mind that every conceivable situation has a wide range of variables (e.g., Who is the attacker? Where are you? What are the circumstances?). This color code does not provide hard lines of action; it simply identifies general categories of human interaction that are helpful in determining the appropriate level of action in the heat of the moment. In general, however, the defender's response should match the attacker's level of intensity. It is important to note that the defender should respond to the level of threat with *assertive,* not aggressive, action. There is a crucial difference between these that will be covered in detail shortly.

Yellow Alert

Yellow alert corresponds to everyday awareness of your surroundings and how you communicate in non-stressful moments. Driving offers a good illustration of this level. You are unconsciously taking in a lot of obvious information (e.g., turn signals, red lights, stop signs, flashing blue lights, and so on) as well as processing a great deal of subtle data, such as the gestures of other drivers' heads, slight movements of other vehicles, your location in a lane or in a city, your speed, the presence of children or dogs near the street, and so on. The same corresponds to self-defense. You should always be aware of the multitude of situations and conditions that present themselves throughout your day. This doesn't mean you need to be hypervigilant or paranoid; it simply means being aware of and alert to what's going on around you.

Orange Alert

The defining line between yellow and orange alert is that point at which you feel any level of threat. In our courses we do a drill where we pair students up to experience the visceral response that occurs when another person abruptly steps into their personal space. It invariably triggers a gut reaction in the person who is being invaded (and some pretty interesting body language). This gut reaction alerts us that the situation has elevated to the next level. It can be triggered by physical proximity, intimidating language, strong or suggestive eye contact, or some other stimulus that you are not even consciously aware of. Gavin De Becker, in his excellent book *The Gift of Fear*, speaks at length on the power of the subconscious to pick up danger signals. Very often we are not consciously aware of a threat, but subconsciously the brain and body are. This is intuition. We all have it, and it is there for no other reason than to help us. Stories abound of people who have an intuitive alarm go off and either don't listen to it or talk themselves out of it, and sure enough, something bad happens. The bottom line here is that any time you feel that panic button go off, or the hairs on the back of your neck stand up, or any other alarm signal your body gives, listen to it! It only happens in response to something, whether conscious or not, and it always has your best interest at heart.

Red Alert

Red alert denotes a situation where an aggressor is, for whatever reason, on the verge of physically attacking you. You are now the proverbial cat in the corner squaring off with the angry dog. The primary difference between orange alert and red alert is that in orange there is still a chance—even if it's a remote one—of de-escalating the situation and leaving peaceably. In red alert, however, the attacker is clearly so incensed that he/she no longer can listen to reason. This is a very volatile situation and will usually come to a fight if it is not dealt with quickly and effectively.

COMMON MISTAKES OF COMMUNICATION

One of the most powerful of all self-defense skills that you can learn is assertive communication. If you just don't communicate that you are an easy victim, you've won more than half the battle right there. This begins with developing an awareness of how you are walking, standing, and the myriad other means of communication that can either entice or discourage a potential predator. Multiple studies show that more than 90 percent of communication consists of body language, facial expression, eye contact, and tone of voice. This means the actual words you speak account for less than 10 percent of communication.

Attackers are experts at watching body language to discern whether you are a good potential victim or not. Almost invariably, predators are looking for the proverbial easy victim. There are powerful correlations between human behavior and that of predators in the animal realm. When a mountain lion goes hunting for dinner, it doesn't go after the biggest, toughest doe or buck in the forest. It goes for the small, weak, sick, easy victim. So it is with human predators when they go looking for their "lunch." Most do not want a real fight but the sense of power they get from prevailing over someone else. Thus, it is not the challenge of the fight that motivates them but the final result.

The typical attacker is a disempowered individual looking for a sense of power and control of his life through acts of violence and coercion. My RMCAT partner, Peyton Quinn, shot some video of personal interviews conducted at a prison in California that corroborates this theory perfectly. Over and over these convicted felons, murderers, burglars, and so on said that they would not target a person who showed any propensity to fight back or give a struggle. They also stated that if a potentially good victim suddenly switched to a defiant demeanor, they would most often back away and call off the attack.

Although there are certainly some attackers out there who are truly vicious sociopathic killers and won't hesitate to go after the biggest and baddest guy in the bar, they represent a very small minority. Crime statistics show that 2 to 5 percent of the population falls into this "dangerous sociopath" category. Furthermore, most predators are not the monstrous behemoths of our overactive imaginations. U.S. Department of Justice statistics indicate that the average attacker is approximately five-foot-six and less than 160 pounds. When you factor in the reality that predators typically don't want to fight, the chances of a determined defense succeeding are quite good if you have the right awareness skills and ability to stand up to the threat.

After 17 years of working with a wide variety of students and having listened to stories galore of real-life altercations, I have come to this conclusion: in an intense situation, if the intended "victim" just doesn't screw up, things typically tend to turn out okay. In other words, if the defender can stay calm and conscious and not go into some emotional knee-jerk response that communicates the wrong message to the potential attacker, the situation usually ends up without anyone getting hurt. But under duress, when the brain gets fuzzy and adrenaline and fear take over, people often screw up and make the situation worse for themselves. In FAST Defense I use a simple, junior high school health class model of passive and aggressive knee-jerk behavior to illustrate just how these screw-ups often occur.

Passive Communication

Nobody wakes up in the morning and says, "Gee, I think I'll go about my day looking and acting like a total victim and see how many predators I can attract." Yet a high percentage of the population does just that unconsciously. Simply being aware of this common communication style can be enough to stop it. *Fake it until you make it* is a very apt principle to follow here. In fact, the very act of changing your body language will usually change your emotional state. Standing, walking, and talking stronger will make you feel stronger.

Classic passive communication.

Since more than 90 percent of communication is body language, this presents important information to both the potential victim and attacker alike. Weak body language, a scared facial expression, lack of eye contact, and mousy tone of voice are flashing green lights for the would-be attacker in selecting a victim. Often a simple look in the eyes, good body posture, or assertive tone of voice is enough for them to leave someone alone and go off in search of an easier victim. There are plenty of them out there.

Aggressive Communication

Aggression is a very real and growing problem in our society. We live in a fast-paced, stressed-out world where pressures abound. It doesn't take much to put many of us over the edge. Push the right button on someone, and you can have an instant raging fire to deal with. Aggression typically manifests itself through one of two channels: macho attitude and triggered anger.

Macho Attitude

One way that people get into real trouble all the time is through cocky bravado, or overreacting. In such cases the victim gets triggered, fires up, and often exacerbates the situation, escalating it when it may not even be necessary. Unfortunately, the cocky response is very common in today's world. Men are constantly bombarded with visions of macho attitude and what it means to be "cool." This can also be termed the "peacock effect," where the person exhibiting the aggression is really scared but doesn't want to show it. It is a very common guy thing, but it is also a growing problem with females. In fact, girls are fighting girls more than boys are fighting boys in junior highs and high schools around America. Women of drinking age are also making "catfights" in bars a much more common occurrence than ever before.

These reactions are a conditioned response to fear and are often quite unconscious. I used to stand door-checking IDs at a bar in a college town and would watch groups of guys walking down the streets all the time. For the most part, these were normal, nice guys just out for a night on the town. But as soon as they walked through the doors of the bar, a great many of them would puff out their chests and look tough in typical territorial displays of machismo. This "peacock" behavior, which was really very simple animal communication, occurred every night, and most of these kids had no idea they were even doing it. If an altercation broke out, the body language increased, sometimes to the point of being comical. More than once I've seen such macho guys standing chest-to-chest or nose-to-nose and even jumping up and down like roosters in a cockfight before any blows were ever thrown. Often no blows were thrown because most of these guys didn't want to fight anyway. They merely got caught up in their conditioned macho crap and were actually relieved when we intervened and broke it up.

Classic aggressive macho behavior.

Clearly, when an aggressor is puffing up like this, it is an effort to cover up his fear. If he were not afraid, he wouldn't have any need for exhibiting all this behavior in the first place. These macho types can usually be pretty easily assuaged by giving them some "props" or using humor in a nonembarrassing way. In essence, you want to give the person an easy out so he can save face. Do this, and he will usually calm down rather quickly. Antagonize him, and he may end up fighting you even though it probably wasn't his intention to do so. Many of these types of aggressive assaults are territorial versus predatorial and are directed toward guys. It can usually be a simple matter of giving them what they want, and they will often cool down.

Triggered Anger

This is where something is said or done to "trigger" a genuine pissed-off response. We all have buttons that, if pushed, can send us into that "see-red" state where we just want to go berserk. It happens all the time, and people die every day from this out-of-control rage. As the line goes; "If we are not in control of ourselves, someone else can be." Many assailants are experts at finding triggers or "buttons" and pushing them, knowing that once their victims lose it they are much easier to control.

Various factors come into play to determine what someone's personal trigger may be. Sometimes it can be a single word. A good friend of mine grew up in New York City, where if anyone ever called you "sport," as in, "How ya doin' there, Sport?" the fight would be on. Ridiculous as most would consider it, "sport" was a culturally conditioned trigger in his part of the world. I have no doubt that people died over the years as a result of action triggered by this and various other words. Epithets like "bitch" and the "C" word for women, the "N" word for African-Americans, and a hundred others fall into the same category.

I was teaching at a well-known martial arts school a while back, and one of the head instructors was an African-American guy. While driving our team from the airport to the training center, this gentleman (whom I will call Bob), knowing that we would be doing realistic verbal provocation on all the students, politely asked us not to use the "N" word on him in any scenario. His worry was that he would go berserk in front of his students, as he had done in real-life street fights where local neo-Nazi gangs had used this word against him. We agreed to honor his request, though we also explained that the very reason we did these verbal scenarios was to break any preconditioned knee-jerk triggers that the bad guys can use on us. Although it might be uncomfortable to play out this scenario, it would be in his best interest to "deprogram" himself to not be triggered by this word.

As the training commenced, he ended up giving us permission to use that and any other inflammatory words we felt appropriate to help him and his students. When it was time to do his verbal defense scenario where the students practice using only verbal assertiveness to ward off an attack, I whispered to my fellow instructor Tim Stott (who was up next and a damn fine one at finding and pushing buttons) to push Bob's buttons with strong racial tones. As soon as the "N" word came out, Bob literally froze in his tracks and began to shake with rage, looking like a mountain lion about to pounce on a rabbit. (Bob was a really big guy and former full-contact karate champion, and Tim was knowingly playing with fire!)

The coach/instructor standing behind Bob adroitly reminded him to breathe and not get emotionally hooked by this verbal assault. Bob responded to his coaching (fortunately for Tim) and took a big breath to break his adrenaline-induced spell. In that magic moment where all can either go to hell in a handbasket or not, Bob skillfully de-escalated the situation and ended up backing Tim away without the need for any physical force. Afterward, Bob heartily thanked Tim for not going easy on him and said that he felt like a huge weight was lifted off his massive shoulders through our disarming of the conditioned power this racial slur had long had over him. Similar successes happen in every class, from children dealing with bullies to teenagers to women and men.

Other triggers can be particular physical gestures. Each culture has different methods of clearly expressing negative sentiment. It is important not to get triggered by these gestures in the heat of the moment. (It's also important to be aware of any cultural gestures when traveling to another country. I taught a course in Brazil a number of years ago and almost learned the hard way that the American gesture of "everything's okay" by putting the thumb and index finger together in a circle meant something entirely different in that country. Fortunately, I did it to someone who had lived in the United States and understood my gesture was meant to be positive. It ended up being pretty funny in the moment but could have turned real ugly had I done it to the wrong person.)

Our protective instincts for our children, loved ones, and even pets can be powerful triggers to make us quickly lose control. I tell the story in all my classes of an incident that occurred to me a couple of years back. One snowy Colorado afternoon I was driving my car with my son, who was 5 at the time. It was nearing dusk, and the roads were quite slippery. Suddenly, a big pickup truck next to me moved into my lane, not seeing me in the limited visibility. I swerved to avoid being hit by him, and my car started fishtailing. My adrenaline instantly shot through the roof, and before the car was even back in control, I was cussing out this truck driver for risking harm to my child. Now typically I'm a very laid-back driver and quick to dismiss or avoid a possibly hostile situation. But not this time, as I got hooked by a macho protective instinct for my son. The next thing you know, Mr. self-defense "expert" was racing up next to the truck and hurling every gesture and obscenity I could think of at this guy. I recall a distant voice way in the back of my brain saying, "What the hell are you doing? You are risking the life of the most precious thing in your life by acting this way!" Yet I was so triggered and out of control that reeling myself in wasn't an option.

Fortunately, this guy did the appropriate thing and continued driving on and didn't engage. Finally, I chilled out and got myself back under control, feeling foolish and self-righteous simultaneously (for the moment anyway). In retrospect, this was a valuable experience for me to identify a personal trigger. The protective instinct button is a big one for most of us with anyone we love or care about. Push the mama- or papa-bear button and watch out. Having awareness of this personal button now, I can avoid losing control like I did that day. When a situation triggers my protective instinct, I can quickly take a few deep breaths and bring my brain into the matter instead of spinning out of control in an emotional knee-jerk response that could make the situation worse. Identifying your personal triggers is extremely important and a lifelong practice. Remember, if you are not in control of yourself, someone else can be.

You can analyze and understand just about any altercation that has gone wrong with these two simple yet often destructive modes of passive and aggressive communication. People react with emotional, knee-jerk responses all the time, regardless of intelligence or martial arts training. It happens with adults, and it certainly happens with teenagers and children. Our students state repeatedly that simply having awareness of these two "styles" has helped them to avoid making the same old mistakes they had been making repeatedly. Being conscious of how you communicate to the world is imperative for good self-defense.

Awareness alone can help keep you safe and also provide tools for dealing with all of life's conflicts, big and small. Instead of "screwing up" and going into knee-jerk responses, you are empowered to find a creative and appropriate response to the situation. This isn't only a good way to defend yourself; it's a great way to live life.

Chapter 5

Assertive Communication: Boundary Setting with Eyes, Body, and Voice

Though martial arts and self-defense systems have long sought the very best techniques to defeat any attacker, with some claiming ownership of the "secret" techniques of the masters, common sense and a good dose of experience show that no magic techniques exist that can make someone impervious to attack. The harsh reality is that physical techniques do not necessarily top the list of self-defense skills that will actually help people in a real confrontation.

The fact is that strong communications skills, applied correctly, can back off almost all attackers. To see why this is so, let's revisit the mind-set of the typical predator. Almost invariably, the predator is looking for an easy victim. When a defender turns toward an attacker and presents a determined demeanor through eye contact, assertive body language, and strong verbal communication, conveying the message that he or she will not be "lunch" today, cognitive dissonance occurs in the attacker's mind as things fail to go as planned. In FAST Defense this is what we call setting a good boundary—that is, drawing a line in the sand and backing it up! The ability to set firm boundaries through the use of eye contact, body language, and a powerful voice comprises the most powerful yet underrated set of self-defense skills because it can literally stop most altercations before they become physically violent.

Size is not a major factor in warding off a potentially bigger opponent, either. Think of a cat cornered by a larger and stronger dog. If the cat tries to run out of the corner, it will trigger the dog's chase response and may well end up being lunch. But should the cat turn toward the dog, raise its hackles, let out a powerful hiss, and show paws full of claws, the dog will typically back off if it has any sense. If not, it will probably get a face full of razor-sharp talons and usually regret its ill-advised perseverance. Humans use very similar methods to set boundaries. Like the cat cornered by a dog, you simply need to show a human predator that you are not willing to be his lunch, and this is usually enough to dissuade him from further action.

If your personal space is invaded, the first thing to do if at all possible is reestablish a safe distance. The exact distance of personal space will be different depending on the situation, but for all practical purposes it is at least two arm's lengths, where the attacker cannot easily strike you. When I was a bar-hopping marine, I used to see all kinds of crazy behavior resulting from someone's attempting to invade someone else's space. The passive person would allow the invader easy access and get walked all over or pummeled. The aggressive person would puff up his chest and stand nose-to-nose with the invader. Of course, the latter response is ridiculous and causes a lot of unnecessary fights, but it is a very conditioned behavior among men. Such a situation can only be resolved in one of two ways, and they both stink. One way is for someone to back down and lose face. The other is with a fight. Ideally, you want to have a few more attractive alternatives to these two options. This requires establishing (or reestablishing) a safe distance or boundary.

Boundaries can be set in three specific ways: eye contact, body language, and verbal communication.

EYE CONTACT

At every seminar I teach, someone invariably raises the question of whether and when to make eye contact. There is no single pat answer that can adequately address this excellent question. But there are some good guidelines that, when accompanied by following your gut instinct, can work quite well.

Yellow Alert

In yellow-alert range, my recommendation is to trust your instincts as to whether to make eye contact with someone. Take the example of a street panhandler. Walking down a street where panhandlers hang out is typically not a threatening situation, though you should certainly be practicing good awareness. Sometimes I will make eye contact with a panhandler if I feel that there is no way of ignoring him. In that case I will usually say something engaging like, "How's it going?" Most panhandlers are not bad people and respond amicably when offered respect. If I get the sense that the person is nice, I'll often give him or her some change, and typically the response is one of genuine gratitude. But if I pick up any kind of weird energy, I'll look the panhandler right in the eye and clearly and politely say, "I'm all out of change" or "Sorry, I can't help you out." Because I am straightforward yet not disrespecting, this is almost invariably the end of the situation. If the panhandler continues, a slightly more firm reply of "I really cannot help you" is enough to get the point across. This can be buffered easily with a smile to be less forceful, or made stronger by no smile at all, depending on the need. Good eye contact is made during the entire verbal exchange and is an important part of the message you wish to convey.

There are times that eye contact in yellow alert can escalate the situation. One good example is a woman making eye contact with a man who might be trying to be amorous. If she is not interested, then eye contact might not be a good idea, since it could be misconstrued as a signal that she's interested. However, it's the type of eye contact she chooses to make that's key. Furtive, shy glances will most likely provoke the guy to stronger attempts to connect. But when done well, a good "look that could kill" type of glance usually stops further attempts in their tracks. Another example is a man in a bar making eye contact with another guy from across the room. In this environment, eye contact is easily taken as a challenge. If the response is direct eye contact back (usually combined with a puffed-up chest and raised chin), then get ready for trouble. Such reactive behavior often escalates into a macho confrontation. Many a bar fight has resulted from a single glance erupting into a heated code-red altercation and then physical violence.

However, if the glance is simply avoided and not allowed to trigger the knee-jerk, macho response, trouble can be averted. To take that a step further, I have found that a genuine smile of confidence and friendly nod work amazingly well to disarm the macho jerks of the world. Why would this work, you might ask? These guys are like dogs trying to hook you with their intimidation tactics. If you don't play that game, then their tactics have failed and you have exhibited confident yet nonprovocative behavior. This most often takes the wind right out of their sails because you are presenting in the exact manner that they don't want to see. They know that your getting hooked by them is a sign of weakness. So by not allowing yourself to be hooked, you make it clear that you are the type of person they don't want to run across: someone genuinely confident who can't be controlled.

So in code yellow there are different rules for eye contact, depending on the situation. If you trust your instincts and display assertive behavior, you will probably do just fine.

Orange Alert

My advice is to make eye contact any time you feel any level of threat from someone. Predators choosing their prey look for the fearful response. Lack of eye contact is a show of submissive behavior in the animal kingdom as well as among humans. Convicted felons confirm that eye contact alone can be enough to dissuade them from attacking an intended victim. But again, it must be done in an assertive manner. Weak, furtive glances will incite the predator. On the other hand, glaring, aggressive eye contact may escalate the situation. Assertive eye contact is made with a straightforward facial and eye expression that says, "I see you" without demeaning the other person or conveying any "attitude." With practice, you will be amazed at how powerful the fine art of making eye contact can be.

Since many situations can be de-escalated from orange back down to yellow, you must ascertain where you think your situation is going. If it is a macho jerk trying to hook you, oftentimes the confident smile and nod are enough to deter the threat. Just because your alarm bell has been activated doesn't mean that a soft approach won't work on this person. The hard stare or shoulder nudge in a bar are two situations where I've used this tactic very successfully. Take the shoulder nudge as an example. You are walking toward the crowded bar to get a drink, and someone passing by gives you a deliberate shove into your shoulder. You could do what many do and get all macho and vindictive. We all know where this typically goes. Or in this golden moment you could look the guy right in the eye with a smile and genuinely say, "Sorry, dude." You now have avoided getting hooked (which was probably his intent), and if it was an accident, then you didn't provoke a fight where there didn't need to be one.

In the case of some guy hitting on a woman, the situation could fall into either yellow or orange alert, depending on how threatened she feels. If she does feel afraid of this guy and is in orange alert, the ideal tactic is to let him down without causing him to lose face. Eye contact softened by a smile, along with good verbal skills (e.g., "I appreciate the offer, but I'm happily married"), often works very well. Of course, congruent assertive body language is the key. Many women have never learned how to do this with confidence and thus may convey mixed messages. This isn't to say that some guys don't take no for an answer. But the truth is that congruent eye contact and body language that say, "Thanks but no thanks" usually work. If not, and the guy is really being a pest, the next level is to give that piercing eye contact. Even total silence can very well be enough if it is backed with a look that could melt ice.

Red Alert

A fight is imminent at this level, and the defender will most likely be experiencing the adrenal rush and the biochemical effects that accompany it. Tunnel vision and auditory exclusion can create a load of trouble if you aren't able to deal with and even use them to your advantage in the heat of the verbal exchange. At this level I find it best to drop the gaze from the attacker's eyes to the chest area. This allows you to avoid getting sucked into the aggressor's gaze or getting psyched out. Many a good street fighter has worked his "stare" into a tool for intimidation. Not only can this work against you psychologically, but it can also set you up for a sneak attack. You would be amazed at how easy it is to hold someone's attention on the eyes while slipping a hand into the pocket for a knife or other weapon to thrust into the unwary victim. Add to this the threat of another attacker, and it's easy to become an ambush victim because of red-alert, tunnel-vision eye-to-eye contact.

Focusing on the chest area has a multitude of benefits. By softening the gaze to a broader area of the attacker's body, you reduce tunnel vision and thus see any body movement the attacker might make. Boxers employ such tactics in the ring. The eyes can be used to fake out the opponent and slip in a sneak shot, so by focusing on the chest area you can see the subtle hip and shoulder shifts that must occur when throwing a strike and respond accordingly. Your peripheral vision opens up, enabling you to see the feet of other attackers should they enter into your space. Finally, it can be very disconcerting for the attacker when an intended victim suddenly focuses all of his attention on the chest area and refuses to get hooked by the woof. Most attackers will leave. If they don't, the defender is ready to go to the next stage if necessary.

Again, good eye contact will only appear credible if it is backed up by correct body language. Let's take a look at how body language enters the equation at each of the three threat levels.

BODY LANGUAGE

Body language is an often-subtle yet highly effective way to assertively set a boundary. The various facets of body language that apply to self-defense, including facial expression, hand and arm position, and stance, must all work together in a congruent manner for maximum impact. The following guidelines should help you get a feel for how you can use the body in various ways to communicate that you will not be an easy victim in each of the three levels of alert. One size does not necessarily fit all in this case, so feel free to improvise with what works for you specifically.

Yellow Alert

Yellow-alert body language should be employed as a matter of course the minute you walk out of the door of your house in the morning. It is a way of carrying yourself that conveys confidence without cockiness and awareness without paranoia. Any time you stop and make eye contact or converse with anyone, be aware of how you are standing. One foot should be slightly ahead of the other. I prefer to have my strong leg back, but this is a personal preference. The hands should come up to chest level in a subtle ready position without conveying any

Yellow-alert stance.

readiness. Some people prefer to keep their hands down at their sides. Although I feel this doesn't communicate as well, it works for some people's style. You do not want to have your hands in your pockets, nor do you want them up in fists. Your facial expression should be soft or neutral. Neutral is the name of the yellow-alert game.

Orange Alert

When your internal alarm bell goes off, indicating a possible low- to moderate-level threat, you should assume a slightly stronger stance and settle into it a little deeper, regardless of whether you feel the person can be de-escalated or not. Your front foot should now be a bit more forward of your rear foot than it was previously, and there should also be a bit more lateral space separating your feet. Your torso should lean slightly forward, and your hands should come up into a gentle but firm assertive position that communicates, "Stop." Your facial expression will vary according to what your

Doing it all wrong!

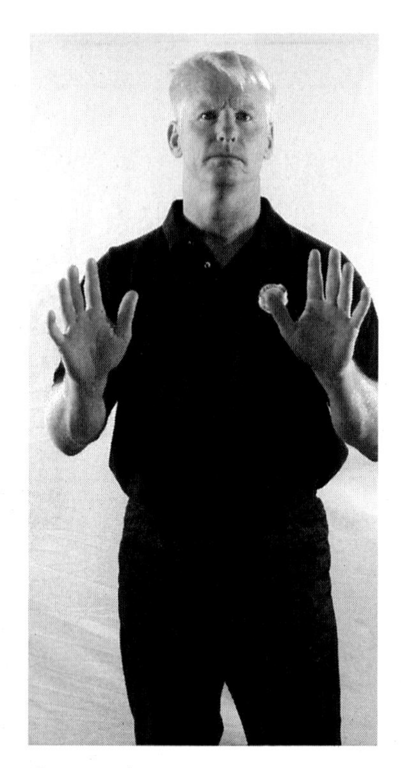

Orange-alert stance.

intuition tells you based on the specific dynamics of the threat: smiling if you are using humor to de-escalate, neutral if you are not sure which way the situation might go, or slightly stern if you want this person to back away.

Red Alert

Should you face someone who is really pissed off and clearly wants to take your head off, it is time to get real assertive real fast, and your body language must back this up. Here you drop into an even deeper stance that clearly communicates a no-nonsense message. Drop your strong

Red-alert stance.

foot back even further behind your front foot and put still more lateral space between them for added stability. (Stay away from any deep martial arts stances, however; not only do they look ridiculous, but they also make it very difficult to move quickly if necessary.) You should be leaning forward even more now and bending more at the knees than the hips. Your hands should be up with the palms facing outward and the fingertips at eye level. Avoid making closed fists, which could escalate the situation. Remember that the red-alert strategy is still aimed at keeping the situation from becoming a fight if at all possible. Your facial expression should convey that you will fight if need be, the objective being to send the person a clear message you are not worth pursuing as a victim.

The final piece of the powerful boundary-setting skill set is verbal defense. When verbal defense is applied congruently with eye contact and stance, it usually precludes the need for any other self-defense techniques because the typical predator will back off when faced with such an assertive response.

VERBAL DEFENSE: THE "SECRET TECHNIQUE"

A few years back, a young karate school owner approached me after I presented the FAST Defense verbal strategies at a large martial arts conference. He very respectfully thanked me for my work and the unique training system I had presented. As he was leaving, he threw me for a loop by saying that in his opinion I was the "toughest guy" he had ever met. Now, although I don't worry about my ability to defend myself, I surely do not consider myself any kind of "tough guy." In fact I try very hard to avoid projecting such an image.

The funny thing is, he made this statement after seeing me do nothing more than talk trash as the woofer bad guy in some live verbal assault scenarios. This drove home the fact that our society often confuses macho jerks with tough guys. Such people need little more than the ability to talk trash to be considered badasses. Society conditions us to believe that talking tough is the same as being tough. In truth, the reverse is usually the case. Think of a dog that goes "WOOF, WOOF" to intimidate its victim into submission. The woof is used to frighten and control and is a condition of fear. If a dog intends to bite someone, it won't announce that intention. It will just go up and bite.

I learned this the hard way, as I do most things. One day I was playing with my son in the home office of a friend. There was a very docile, sweet chocolate Labrador retriever who quietly sat in his corner all day long. Something made me tease it by feigning a growling, movie-style monster attack on my son, assuming the dog would do nothing in response. In a flash I detected a dark form in the air just inches from the right side of my throat. Very luckily, I jerked back and brought my arm up to block the attack. I still carry an impressive scar where that sweet, submissive animal decided a helpless child was worth taking a 110 percent stand for. I never heard a premonitory whimper or growl at all, and I learned a hell of a good lesson.

Human predators work the same way when they really want to cause you serious harm. If a skilled bad guy really has the intention of harming you, most likely he will do so as an ambush or blitzkrieg attack, and the fight will be on (and usually over) very quickly. Although this certainly does happen, as in the case of robberies or drive-by shootings, the majority of assaults are not of this type. It's much more typical that a verbal assault precedes any physical attack. In such cases, the woof is typically nothing more than a fear-based drama intended to get the victim to run away or comply, depending on the situation.

Using the woof to intimidate.

The fact that most attacks on women are successfully executed with nothing more than a verbal threat is a direct result of the socio-conditioning that equates trash talk with being tough and intimidating. The bad guys know this and use their woof successfully over and over because it usually works. Men who are abusing their wives and girlfriends also use the woof to intimidate them into staying in long-term abusive relationships.

The good news is that the woof can be turned to the defender's favor. By deprogramming the cultural conditioning that predisposes people to succumb to a predator's threats, we can neutralize the woofers' power that is so dear to them. Furthermore, by skillfully using a reverse version of the woof, we can capitalize on this same socio-conditioning by turning the woof on the woofer.

Turning the Woof on the Woofer

Half or more of the battle in teaching self-defense is desensitizing students to the verbal trash that many attackers use so effectively. We have been conditioned by society to be polite to others and refrain from using foul language. We are taught not to raise our voices and to display good manners no matter how we are treated by others. Many of us are conditioned to be shocked, or at least feel uncomfortable, when someone uses abusive language, speaks unkindly about us, or violates our comfort zone. The problem is that our discomfort and shock give our enemy a weapon to use against us. Scenario-based training works exceedingly well in disarming the enemy of that weapon.

The first way this occurs is through desensitization to the woof. Most FAST Defense graduates report that they find verbal threats in real altercations much easier to deal with after having taken one of our courses. In fact, many

Using assertive verbal and body language skills to back off a woofer.

students say that the street woofers can't even woof as well as we do in our classes. Secondly, since verbal tactics work so well for the bad guys, scenario-based training can also make verbal skills work quite well for the good guys with a little bit of tweaking. Our graduates report that their newfound verbal skills work like magic when applied correctly, usually circumventing the need for any physical defense at all. Verbal defense is really the optimal technique, and it works amazingly well.

The Color Code of Verbal Defense

Making the appropriate response to a threat at the appropriate time, neither underreacting (passively) nor overreacting (aggressively), is easier said than done when the heartbeat rises, adrenaline begins flooding the neural pathways, and the cognitive parts of the brain begin shutting down as blood rushes from the major organs to feed the muscles for a flight-or-fight response. The ingrained propensity to react in an emotional, knee-jerk fashion is difficult to overcome. Most people do not overcome it and thus get themselves into trouble.

Worse still is reacting out of some of the ridiculous cultural conditioning that tells you how you're supposed to respond to be cool. One myth that has to be debunked is that it's necessary to have a snappy retort or say just the right thing to an attacker. You have probably experienced a hot verbal altercation where words were being tossed around like hot rocks. Then afterward, as you were driving home, you began to think of all the things you "should have said." Well, most likely those things you thought of after the fact would have escalated the situation because their objective was to verbally jab the attacker, which is aggressive behavior. As a kid I used to sit around with my buddies and think of all the good, snappy comeback lines. Funny thing how these pre-planned retorts rarely reached our lips in the adrenaline rush of a real confrontation, and on those occasions that they did, the end result was probably a fight!

Since 90 percent of communication is nonverbal, *how* you say something is much more important than *what* you say. It is important that body language, eye contact, and tone of voice are all congruently assertive.

But how do you know what is the correct level of response so you don't anger the attacker by escalating things—or let the aggressor walk all over you as your brain and body freeze up? This is perhaps the greatest challenge in teaching effective self-defense. To meet that challenge, I use what I call the color code of verbal defense, a simple frame of reference based on the color code of awareness:

- Yellow alert: no or very low level of threat (conversation level)
- Orange alert: moderate level of threat (somewhat heated conversation)
- Red alert: high level of threat (very intense verbal attack on the verge of physical violence)

Bear in mind that these levels are not hard lines meant to be followed as strict rules but rather general guidelines. Every situation is different, with its own unique variables of who, where, and why. Obviously, not every altercation begins at yellow alert and escalates to red. An ambush attack, for instance, will fire up right into red or above. Other altercations may start mid-level and drop down. The color code is a tool that enables people to first identify where they are in any situation at any given point and then respond in an appropriate manner that's congruent to the level of threat. If you can do this, the situation typically turns out okay. Having the skills to avoid an emotional, knee-jerk response gives you the opportunity to engage the brain and find a creative and effective solution to the problem. This three-level verbal defense strategy we teach in FAST Defense provides the defender with a realm of appropriate choices for de-escalating a range of threats, from low-level to very high-level, with the goal of keeping the altercation from becoming physical.

Yellow Alert

Common conversation falls into the yellow-alert category. Most conversation is safe and nonthreatening. However, many predators use conversation as a means to scope out or "interview" a prospective victim to see how he or she will respond. When the victim shows signs of passivity, it allows the predator to take the next step. Therefore, it's good practice to always be aware of how you are communicating when you talk with someone, even if the person is totally harmless. The correct way is to stand upright with your strong foot slightly behind the other so you are centered and strong, make eye contact, and use an assertive, confident tone of voice. You can practice doing this with everyone you come into contact with. If you find it difficult, then your conditioned style of communication is probably more passive, and your challenge is to come out of your shell to become more assertive. If it is too easy, then you may lean more to the aggressive side, and your challenge could be to back off your energy a bit.

Sometimes a predator will bombard you with questions to keep you on the defensive and off guard. Phone solicitors are very adept at this, artfully running the conversation by not letting you get a word in edgewise. The three-level verbal defense strategy taught in scenario-based training empowers people to deal with all sorts of aggressors, from pesky solicitors to aggressive coworkers to dangerous predators. Here is an example of how these skills can be applied with a phone solicitor:

Solicitor: "Hello, is so-and-so there?"
You: "Who's calling please?"
Solicitor: "This is John _ _ _ with so-and-so."
You: "What is this concerning?"
Solicitor: "I am with so-and-so calling for . . ."
You: "Is this a solicitation?" (Just interrupt him if he is getting at all verbose.)
Solicitor: "Yes, so-and-so is so-and-so . . ." (He must, by law, state that it is.)
You: "Thank you, but I'm not interested. Please take

me off your list." (Again, the law requires him to do so if you so ask. Most often solicitors will reply with a scripted response agreeing to take you off and stating that it may take a week or so and thank you. Or they may just hang up in frustration).

The same tactic for taking control of the conversation works very well with a potential predator. In yellow alert you often have the chance to avoid the person entirely. If you can simply walk on by, then you should do so. At the same time, you have to be careful not to portray yourself as the cat running out of the corner. If you try to walk by this person and sense any threat at all, the best thing is to turn to him and deal head-on with the situation. This is a conscious, active response as opposed to a passive response where you continue walking, turning your back on them and basically giving them the power to make the next move.

The key in human interaction is whether you make the *choice* to connect with someone or not. An appropriate response to a given situation comes from a skillful and conscious mind-set, not from fear-based avoidance or a forced connection with someone you really don't want to talk to. If you choose not to engage because you feel something is amiss about this person then honor that feeling and respond accordingly. If you choose to connect with the person, then do so appropriately. Remember that the yellow-alert level of this scale corresponds to a non-threatening level of interaction. This doesn't mean that the person may not be interviewing you to be a victim, but nevertheless the situation still has not escalated to the orange "be on alert" level that I will describe shortly.

If the person is asking you something, I suggest answering the first few questions, since most people are not predators interviewing you as a victim. If he asks for directions, provide them. If he is panhandling, trust your gut feeling about whether you choose to help him out. If he doesn't leave, or if you feel uncomfortable and feel the encounter has gone on long enough, you can take control by asking, "what do you want?" or "what can I do for you?" or "what do you need?" It is important to do this with a normal tone of voice, not with aggressive attitude and not with a wimpy, passive voice. Now the tables are turned because you have answered a question with a question. If you do it with assertive energy, most predators will leave you alone right there. If not, then it will probably trigger your alarm buttons and escalate the situation to orange-alert level, requiring more assertiveness on your part.

Orange Alert

If the invader continues to push into your space, a much more assertive demeanor and verbal defense are required to maintain good distance. This doesn't necessarily mean a fight has to happen. I break orange alert into two phases.

The lower orange-alert level allows possible peaceful resolution. I have found a little humor and even assertive humility go a long way in diffusing a hot situation. I have even ended up buying a beer for people and, on very rare occasions, even become friends with them after dealing with them skillfully at this level.

However, if the invader is pushing really hard, I'll only back up once or twice before assuming a strong stance and issuing a verbal command of "Stay back!" or something similar. At this point it is a no-nonsense situation and must be conveyed as such. Many people might consider this an aggressive response. My retort is that it's not *what* you say nearly so much as *how* you say it. Most people respond with major attitude or even aggressiveness in their voice and body language. It is very different to assert yourself with a solid hands-up stance and what my friend and fellow bulletman Mike Haynack calls the "bad dog" voice. The tone of voice is very important and is indeed the same one used when admonishing a dog that has misbehaved. A no-nonsense, commanding tone of voice without aggressiveness or attitude works amazingly well for canines and humans alike.

Red Alert

If the previous techniques did not work and the aggressor is clearly on the verge of attacking you, what you say is not as important for the attacker as it is for possible witnesses. At this point the attacker will be so incensed that he will have auditory exclusion and won't hear much of what you are saying anyway, though he surely will be reading your other methods of communication. If you are in a public place, be aware that witnesses also experience the effects of the adrenal rush and tend to have very selective memory that could work against you, even when you are the defender. In order to cover yourself later should the situation become physical, stay away from inflammatory remarks, cursing, or macho threats. Be careful to stay away from all those clever retorts that can escalate the situation or make you look like the aggressor. Saying things like, "Back away, I don't want to fight you!" with a strong bad dog voice works best. Your tone of voice and body language will convey the message to the attacker, and witnesses are more likely to remember that you "didn't want to fight."

Many people view this strategy as dangerous, fearing that it could piss off the attacker even more. Bear in mind that we are not taking this level of response unless the attacker is already on the verge of becoming physically violent. Do you think the cat in the corner is more worried about making the dog angry, or doing everything it can to keep the dog from eating it for breakfast? This is a last-ditch effort to back the assailant away and avoid physical violence. It almost always works.

If the situation is extremely intense, one creative strategy is to loudly say to the attacker, "I see the knife! Put the knife down!" Not only will this get the attacker's attention and very possibly break his mind-set (whether he has a knife or not), but think of what the witnesses will remember if interviewed by the police. Most likely they will state, "He had a knife!" even if he did not. This strategy can't hurt you and could very well help you a great deal.

The vast majority of our students who use verbal defense find that the yellow- and orange-level responses are quite effective in diffusing most situations. This is consistent with our knowledge of the mind-set of predators: they are looking for the easy victim and will typically back off when things do not go right for them. Nevertheless, our students have the conditioned ability to take the verbal strategy to code-red level if necessary. Rarely will the situation continue toward physical violence if red-alert verbal boundaries are applied correctly. If it does, the adrenaline is already working in the defender's favor, and it's a matter of taking it to the next step, which is physical defense (the subject of the next chapter).

Territorial vs. Predatorial Attacks

Although the basic dynamics of defense for both women and men are more alike than not, there are some important differences. Most women are attacked predatorily—that is, the assailant is looking to get something from the victim. Although this also happens to men, we most often deal with territorial situations where the intention is simply to get us out of the attacker's "turf," whatever that may be.

The significance of the territorial attack is that the aggressor will usually give you some sort of an "out." It's imperative, then, that you do not let auditory exclusion tune out what the attacker is saying so you can determine whether a way out is being presented. Applying the assertive bad dog voice in a territorial situation can be like throwing gas on a fire. The best response is to soften eye contact and tone of voice and comply if at all possible. It is better to leave and possibly lose face than to macho it out and lose a whole lot more. Only if compliance is not possible should you adopt the "cat in the corner" strategy.

Territorial—if they give you a chance to leave, take it!

Determining whether a situation is predatorial or territorial can be quite a challenge in the middle of a heated and scary situation. Sometimes a situation might start out as predatorial and change to territorial. In our classes we put our students through various situations that condition them to determine the type of assault they are experiencing and the appropriate response.

* * *

When you consider that most altercations occur in the lower yellow and orange levels, it is clear that verbal skills are the most important to effective self-defense and the most appropriate way to go in most cases. Yet they are the most difficult to master because of societal conditioning. For most of our students, practicing these skills is the most challenging part of our classes. They would usually rather hit the aggressor than verbally back him off. But it is the verbal defense skills that will work to keep almost any situation from becoming violent.

How unfortunate that the vast majority of self-defense instruction focuses on defensive techniques to use once the fight has started rather skills that will almost always prevent the fight from happening in the first place!

Chapter 6

Physical Defense: It's Not the Size of the Dog in the Fight . . .

Although the concepts of FAST Defense training can be modified to work with almost any particular group, the physical techniques addressed in this book are best applied to the general self-defense market. They are not designed to make professional fighters, bouncers, law enforcement agents, bodyguards, or military special ops hand-to-hand combat experts. They are simple and easy for anyone to learn. In fact, any martial arts student typically learns them in the first month or so of training.

The golden rule for general self-defense is that physical defense is only to be used when all else has failed. FAST Defense is not about training people to escort a drunken fool out of a bar or restrain a burglar or knock out a well-trained opponent in a ring. It is about training people to deal appropriately with a real-life threat that is scaring the hell out of them, using every possible means to de-escalate or deter the attacker and then, *only* when all else fails, flipping the switch and fighting for themselves like demons possessed.

Physical defense is not a game at this point. It is all-out survival. Experience has shown again and again that the adrenal rush is so intense in real altercations that complex thinking and fine motor dexterity go right out the window. The techniques that work consistently are simple gross motor strikes focused to vulnerable areas on the attacker's body. The number-one factor in whether a defender wins an altercation is the ability to deal with and use the adrenal rush—not the ability to execute fancy karate or kung-fu techniques! Although a well-trained martial arts master may be able to pull off deadly tornado kicks or other complicated moves, it is absolutely unrealistic to teach the average person to do so.

Research has shown that the part of the brain that is functioning under severe distress can only handle about five bits of information. Applied to self-defense, that means a well-trained person can apply a maximum of about five techniques in a real altercation. To put this into perspective, professional boxers typically use only three to four techniques in an entire fight. So even in a prearranged combative situation, things must be kept simple to be effective. In real fights, which happen very quickly, someone who has learned a thousand and one fancy techniques cannot apply more than a few of them at best. Someone with no training at all will either flail ineffectually or freeze up completely.

Proficiency in a technique is secondary to the ability to apply that technique under duress. This can be frustrating for martial artists, who rely on years of intensive training to pull off the great moves we see in the movies. It was damn frustrating for me. Years of martial arts and military special forces training still didn't train me to look like Bruce Lee did in his movies. Every fight I was involved in or witnessed was wild and crazy, and all that fancy movie stuff went out the window in a heartbeat. Yet that cool-as-ice robotic cinematic image was what I strove for, and I figured it would simply take more years of training to accomplish. This was not to be.

Instead, it took years for me to learn that the real challenge for defenders who are forced into a physical defense situation is to find the power necessary to damage the attacker enough to escape or survive. In the adrenal rush, all physical movements speed up and shorten up. This fact, misunderstood or ignored in most self-defense and martial arts training, warrants repeating: *in the adrenal rush, physical movements speed up and shorten up*. In terms of defensive action, this equates to classic choppy, erratic, flailing movements, and it occurs even in people with extensive martial arts training. In fact, based on my work with more than 1,000 martial artists, including many high-ranking masters and even former world champions, I have drawn the unpopular conclusion that most martial arts training causes martial artists to flail more than folks who have no such training.

This is a result of sparring and tournament fighting, where contact is either prohibited or extremely restricted to ensure the safety of the participants. Such training develops great speed and control, but under duress, where each movement speeds up and shortens up, this can actually be a detriment, resulting in a series of very quick strikes with limited power. Power is further reduced by the muscle memory developed from pulling punches in training and tournament fighting to avoid hurting an opponent or drawing a disqualification. Martial artists typically experience an initial frustrating hump in our courses as they retrain new muscle memory that enables them to slow down enough to get maximum power.

A fight is nothing more than one strike at a time. Anything more than that typically manifests as flailing. Think about hammering a nail. An unskilled person will hit too fast and out of rhythm, working like hell and getting nowhere with the nail. A skilled carpenter will drive the nail all the way down with one powerful stroke. There is a preferred rhythm of a sort in a fight, where the skilled defender can literally control the tempo with maximum power, timing, and speed. Most fights are crazy and wild, with few shots ever really hitting well. I have seen gang fights where very little damage was ever sustained because of the wild, unfocused hits. Again, everything speeds up and shortens up under duress.

The trick is to find the ideal combination of speed and power for maximum effect. This usually means slowing down enough so that maximum power can be found. Most martial artists think I'm nuts when I explain this to them in class (usually the ones who have never been in real fights). They have trained forever with maximum speed in complex combinations and have come to depend on these for some possible future defense. Often their first fight against the bulletman is very unsatisfying because he will not react to weak or ineffective strikes, no matter how fast they come. Only when he receives one or more focused, powerful strikes will he respond accordingly. Typically, these students quickly see the point of power versus speed and adjust quite well.

To sum up the merits of physical defense as succinctly as possible, in a physical confrontation the crazier person wins. Pretty profound, eh? Think about it. Have you ever tried to hold a cat that really did *not* want to be held? Was the cat focusing on sensitive nerve points and fancy joint manipulations? Hell no. A cat goes wild, scratching and biting anything it can, and anyone with any sense is going to let that cat loose as fast as possible. The same is definitely true with humans. I remember one day long ago, when I was antagonizing my little brother mercilessly over some ridiculous thing or another. He was intimidated because I was much older, bigger, and stronger than he was. It shocked me to the core when he figured he had finally had enough of my crap and went berserk on me. I reared back in amazement as the wild-eyed little maniac turned on me with a startling ferociousness. Not only did he get me to stop harassing him that day, but I never did it to him again.

Even the most determined attacker will usually back off against a spirited all-out defense. When you consider the fact that most attackers are not looking for a fight, the odds are greatly in the defender's favor, regardless of the physical techniques used. The martial techniques are simply the physical expression of the defender's fighting spirit. They should be simple enough to be implemented by someone who does not necessarily have greater strength than his or her attacker, and they should be focused to vulnerable areas of the attacker's body. Any technique that requires a lot of thinking or physical dexterity is simply ineffective.

Again, I want to make it clear that I am not slamming martial arts. There are any number of good martial arts styles and instructors who can teach effective self-defense. Likewise, a whole slew of strikes have the potential to be employed effectively in an altercation. I am simply pointing out that there are gaps between traditional martial arts training and the reality of combat. In FAST Defense we strive to create a bridge—the crucial missing link that enables martial artists to apply what they've learned in the dojo to real-life encounters in the streets. We also operate on the theory that people can be trained to defend themselves very effectively without years of martial arts training.

In FAST Defense we keep the strikes as simple as possible so the defender does not have to think any more than necessary. By not staying in the conscious mind in an effort to determine which technique to apply to what target, our students are able to focus on utilizing the power of unimpeded adrenaline. People who remain technique-minded tend not only to miss the opportunity to execute their fancy technique but also, more importantly, to inhibit the sheer power of adrenaline to do the job. Self-defense experts always say you must react instantly without thinking, yet most have no practical method of actually teaching people how to do this, aside from endless repetition (which has been shown to be marginally effective at best). FAST Defense training is designed to work using the primitive parts of the brain and exploiting the power of fear and adrenaline as an ally, not an impediment. Teach the part of the brain that will function under duress, and it will respond accordingly.

The following physical techniques are derived from Matt Thomas' initial research and subsequent years of trial and error. Although there have been modifications over the years, the techniques taught in adrenal stress response training still remain much the same because they were founded on sound principles and have proven themselves through real-life success stories over three decades.

STANCE

Most combat stances are . . . well, combat stances. In FAST Defense, we don't use formal martial arts stances that could tip off an attacker to our ability to fight. This gives us the advantage of surprise if a situation does turn physical. The stance has to look natural, so we use what could be called a "stop walk" stance with weight adjustments that are almost invisible except to the well-trained eye. We are all pretty good at walking at this point in our lives, and if we take a step and stop, our bodies should be in a pretty stable position. Distributing the weight 60 percent on the balls of the feet and 40 percent on the heels and having both knees bent, pelvis tucked, is the most efficient ready position for forward movement. Tilting the pelvis slightly forward allows the spinal column and abdominal wall to transfer rotation and counterforce rotation with the resultant momentum from the thighs, glutes, and calves to the upper torso, the basis of Bruce Lee's one-inch punch. It also causes the abdominal muscles to contract to protect the internal organs. In addition to looking natural, the stance also *feels* natural, which is highly practical. In all the fights I have experienced, never once did I stop to think of dropping into one of the many traditional martial arts stances I have learned over the years.

A proper stance should show confidence but not cockiness.

HAND POSITION

In the original Model Mugging program, Matt Thomas modified the inside block from Shotokan karate to include open hands with a 180-degree outward rotation to block incoming strikes with the outside forearms while going into the defensive stance. In this variation, the forearms and elbows are bent at 90 degrees, not too far extended and not too close to the chest, similar to the "unbendable arm" of aikido. It is also a double block, protecting both sides of the head and chest as well as the midline. As an added bonus, this arm position allows escapes from holds that will work whether the attacker grabs the defender with his thumb inside or outside the defender's wrists. Because it forces an isometric chest and back muscle lock, this is also the strongest way for the body to brace itself for a forward hard impact against a wall or the floor. Although it is a combat stance, the open hands are the universal sign of neutrality and can

Proper hand position.

often be enough to de-escalate a situation before physical defense becomes necessary.

I have done experiments with this hand position as a defensive posture against the most common punches and strikes used in real fights. Having the hands in this position makes it remarkably difficult for someone to hit you, with no additional fancy blocks whatsoever being required. FAST Defense physical tactics are based on entering and striking, so this position protects the head while setting up the body to strike quite well.

THE VOICE

Another innovation Matt came up with was a new twist on the *kiai,* or martial arts "shout," in order to make optimal use of the awesome power of the voice. In essence, Matt translated the *kiai* into English, or whatever the primary attacker's language might be, so that it was accessible to the average person rather than having some obscure Asian meaning. The Model Mugging *kiai* was "NO!" First of all, it means "NO!" and many people are conditioned to stop whatever they are doing when they hear it.

If done as a low-pitched roar, it is also animal communication, expressed as a growl or threat. If unexpected, it can cause the "startle" or freeze response in many predatory mammals who were expecting easy prey. The auditory startle response in most primates causes them to spread their legs for better balance (which opens the groin up as a target), put their arms out for better balance (which opens the centerline to become a better target), crouch for better balance (which lowers the head as a target), hunch their shoulders (which weakens the arms toward the midline and opens the throat as a target), and inhale (which makes the ribs easier to break). For millions of years, primates were attacked mainly from the rear by either large felines or other primates, so the ability to freeze to hear better, spread their weight in order to pivot in any direction, and listen for the next clue was critical to survival!

At the same time, exhaling air forcefully causes the rib muscles to contract, protecting the lungs. The abdominal muscles also contract, protecting internal organs, and the pectoral and latissimus muscles contract to help compress the ribs, which also tightens the arm position and focuses the attention forward.

The "NO!" is a powerful war cry to launch a fierce attack and helps focus one's energy toward the attacker. After Barry French made the first impact meters available to martial artists on a large scale, Matt found that his students hit about 25 to 35 percent harder if they yelled as they struck. It can also attract a lot of attention, which most assailants do not want. And unlike a whistle, which must be accessed, put to the lips, and blown, the voice is always with the defender. Most importantly, in my experience, the yell counters the most common problem people have under duress: holding their breath. The freeze-or-flail response occurs as a result of holding the breath, which constricts the entire body, locking the hips and causing upper body flailing and, in the worse case, total freeze-up. Conversely, a powerful exhale allows maximum force with the body and promotes maximum spirit.

STRIKES

The strikes we teach in our FAST Defense Basics course are palm-heels, knees, stomps, slaps, and elbows. Front kicks, although a great technique, are not taught at the basics level for a couple of reasons. For students with no martial arts training, the front kick is more difficult to apply than the knee strike and could get them into trouble if used improperly. Those who have studied martial arts will tend to stay out in sparring distance and not commit to the enter-and-strike tactics we employ, and ruling out front kicks helps to break them of that tendency. Most real attacks get very close in no time, and you can quickly lose the advantage by trying for a late front kick instead of closing with a crunching knee. This is not to say that simple kicks won't work. I have personally used front kicks very effectively against real attacks, but for the reasons stated I choose to reserve them for advanced courses.

Palm-Heel Strikes

Many martial styles teach closed-fist strikes to the head. After learning from experience, I do not advocate hitting to the head with a closed fist. Although you might hit the guy just right and knock him down or out, the little bones in the hand and wrist very often lose to the big bones of the skull. I have broken fingers against opponents' heads, and it is not a good thing. The most common injury with boxers is a broken hand, even with extensive wraps and gloves. In one class I fought a pro boxer from the Netherlands who hit my helmet with closed punches despite repeated warnings not to. He broke his hand in the first hit and kept on hitting because he was so adrenalized. His hand had several broken bones by the time the fight was over. The good thing was that he never felt the break during the fight. The bad thing was that he required some heavy surgery to remedy the problem. A good rule of thumb is to hit hard against soft and soft against hard (as in a punch to the stomach or a palm-heel strike to the head).

In FAST Defense we strike with the open heel of the palm. The palm-heel strike from wing chun is a strong, close-range technique that can be learned easily and safely. Because it is linear, the palm-heel can cover the longest distance in the shortest amount of time.

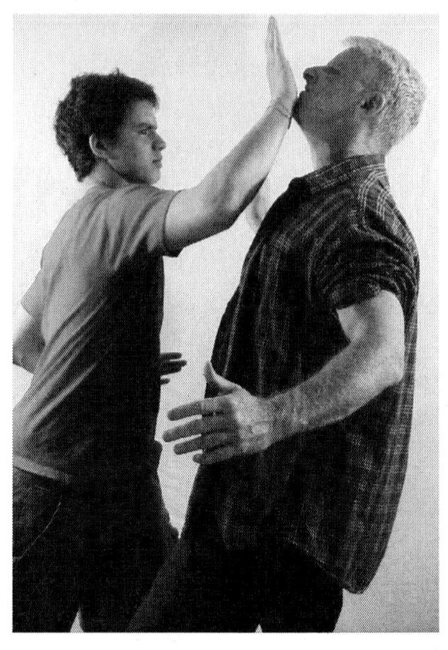

Palm-heel strike.

The palm-heel strike is aimed at the bridge of the nose. If it connects, it can easily break the delicate bones, causing pain, plentiful tears (which produce temporary blindness), and even a knockout in some cases. If it misses to one side and hits an eye, it will cause pain in that eye, which generates sympathetic tears in the other eye, and again, if forceful enough, it can cause a knockout. If it misses low, it will hit the lower portion of the nose and upper teeth, causing pain, sympathetic tears, and possibly a knockout. If it misses high, it will at least tilt the head back, and then as the head rebounds, it will be coming toward a second palm-heel strike.

Since Matt's first courses were just for women, he naturally looked to wing chun, which, according to legend, was designed by a woman for women. Because women statistically have narrower shoulder widths than men, they have to get in close and control the centerline. The proximity of the vital targets of the eyes, nose, throat, and groin to the centerline make the palm-heel strike particularly advantageous to women. The woman's defensive stance protects her own centerline, and if she can get inside her opponent's guarding limbs, she can rapidly fire offensive strikes, forcing the opponent to react with defensive moves before he can launch offensive counterattacks.

For the purposes of FAST Defense, I have modified the palm-heel strike to work for both men and women by employing a larger lateral movement in the hips than was originally taught to me. The hips are the power center of the body. Since there is a strong proclivity to lock the hips in the adrenal rush, a rotation of the hips creates more power more easily, especially for smaller people. With the right training, students of all sizes can quickly learn to hit this way with amazing power. When that power is combined with the proper timing and warrior spirit, we bulletmen really get our bells rung from these strikes, even when protected by 10-pound helmets. (This prompted me to develop a whole series of dynamic blocks for use within the body armor so as to prevent the bulletmen from sustaining permanent brain injury from our students' focused counterattacks!)

Knee Strikes

Striking with the knee is a very easy technique to learn that works quite well at the close proximity at which most fights occur. It also works regardless of the defender's size and strength because it uses the larger leg muscles and the hard surface of the knee to strike vulnerable targets on the attacker's body. In FAST Defense we work off the concept that the leg that is back is the power side, the one that can deliver strikes with the most force. Thus we use the rear leg to deliver the knee strike

A properly executed knee strike with hands in protective position.

to whatever target we are aiming for. Driving off the ball of the foot, the defender leads with the knee, toes pointed down to the ground (pulling the toes back constricts the calf muscles and inhibits range of motion), while throwing the same-side hip into the strike. Ideally, it is the lower portion of the thighbone, *not* the knee, that is actually used to strike upward and crush the opponent's testicles against his own pelvic bone. We teach students to drive the knee up to the height of their own chest, even though an opponent's testicles are usually a lot lower. Driving forward also adds the momentum of the body movement to the strike.

Since most men's reaction to getting kneed in the groin is to clutch the groin and double over in pain, the head naturally drops down. So if the defender remembers to keep his or her palms up following the kick, the attacker will likely head-butt himself on the palm-heel, in essence giving the defender a free follow-up strike with the hand.

Stomps

A good stomp on the instep or toes with the hard ball of the heel is a great technique should you be grabbed from behind in a bear-hug type of attack. This requires little dexterity or fine motor control and can be accomplished even if you cannot see the target. Raking the heel or side of your foot down along the shin of the attacker is another great way to go. It would take a very determined attacker to continue holding on while you smashed his feet or scraped his shin. At the least you are giving him a lot to think about and inhibiting his ability to continue his attack.

Slaps

Another great technique to use while in a rear bear hug is the slap to the groin. We call this a "can opener" in that it's not intended to be a show stopper (though it can be if executed with full power). It is meant to loosen the attacker's grasp so that you can execute a power strike. Men are very hardwired to protect their groins, and any "activity" in that area will elicit a reaction. Few men will stand there taking such strikes and not loosen their grips or let go completely. If they do not, then just hit them harder. The slap is executed from a bent forward position acquired by slamming your butt against his pelvis. The hands should be up in protective position similar to the red-alert stance, to protect your face should you go down to the ground. This also prevents him from trapping your hands down by your side. The elbows are locked in by your sides, and the open palms face outward. The hands arch forcefully down toward the attacker's groin, while the hip rotates with the strike for more power and greater clearance to the target. The great thing about this strike is that even if your arms are pinned at your side, you can still get a flicking motion or even a good grab onto the testicles. Once the attacker lets go, the elbow is often a perfect follow-up strike.

Elbows

The rear elbow, executed correctly, can be a clean knockout strike. It comes fast and very straight back from the defender into the attacker. It is ideal to launch the elbow strike with the strong-side arm (the one on the side of the leg that is back). The motion is much like reaching forward to grab the starter cord of a lawn mower and pulling that cord straight back behind you. Pivoting the hips and feet toward the attacker lends the strike extra power and range. A linear strike straight toward the attacker is better than a circular one, which lacks the range. You don't want to swing and miss this great opportunity to stop the attacker in his tracks.

The forward elbow is a personal favorite and is also very powerful when correctly applied. Getting into the very close range that is required for this strike to enter and destroy does require an extreme level of commitment. Most people tend to want to stay back a bit and not commit so fully, so they miss out on the power that this technique can create. But when done well, this is a devastating strike that can break ribs or knock someone silly almost no matter where you hit them. For this strike, the strong-side hand is in a fist with thumb and forefinger placed against your chest above the solar plexus. The hips and elbow rotate forward together as you lean into the strike and drive the elbow into the target. This is a fun one to practice against a heavy bag or speed bag. But be very aware that under duress, you have to get much closer than you would think to land this powerhouse.

TARGET AREAS

When Matt was first figuring out which anatomical targets to focus on in Model Mugging, he took a one-pound weight and dropped it from the height of one foot to generate a foot-pound of energy. Since kinetic energy is mass times velocity squared, speed can liven up the effect considerably. Matt lay down and dropped the weight on his skull, cheek, chin, temple, and so on, and felt no real pain. Nonetheless, even he was not crazy enough to drop it on his eyes, nose, teeth, or Adam's apple. Next he dropped it on his chest, arms, legs, and so on. Again, no pain. When he lay down and dropped the weight on his groin, it was uncomfortable because it hit his penis, causing pain, but it was still bearable. However, when he spread his legs, lifted his hips and dropped it on his testicles, he decided, "To hell with science; that hurt enough."

Even a small student can easily generate 60 to 100 foot-pounds of energy with the palm-heel strike and from 200 to 400 foot-pounds of energy with a rising knee. As a bulletman, I have been taking strikes in the body armor for 17 years as of this writing and am still going strong. In fact, the growing popularity of FAST Defense training has me in the suit more than ever before as I travel worldwide training new instructors. Believe me when I say that I personally appreciate Matt's willingness to donate his body to the science of self-defense so that the rest of us could carry on the good work. Talk about the school of hard knocks!

In truth, there is no *bad* target if a person fights with total conviction. The best strategy in a fight is a sustained attack to any parts of the attacker's body that present themselves. In FAST Defense we are not about teaching a single beautiful strike to the perfect target where you then stand back and admire your handiwork. Although most attackers back off rather quickly after a good strike (if they choose to fight at all after verbal defense is employed), the truth is that there are human monsters out there that you really do not want to fight against. But if fight you must, total fighting spirit focused into repetitive strikes is definitely your best chance for coming out on top.

That said, some targets are certainly better than others. In FAST Defense we focus on the primary targets of the head and groin, and anything else (e.g., ribs/solar plexus, knees, feet) serves as brownie points on the way to one or the other. Since we are only fighting as a last resort, a sustained and committed attack is emphasized more than striking to a single target area and hoping it will have the desired effect.

Head

The head is a great target area. Notice I say "the head" and not "pressure point GB 18" or some other specific area. Hitting a moving target the size of a head is hard enough in the heat of battle, much less some tiny point somewhere. However, there are general target areas on the head that work better than others, and those are eyes, nose, jaw, and throat.

Eyes

The eyes are exceptional targets because we humans are hardwired to protect them. One of my female students realized this firsthand many years ago. She was halfway through a two-part class, and we had let the students practice eye strikes against the armored assailant, using the voice when striking to break the freeze response, provide greater power, and even scare the attacker. She went home that Saturday evening to an empty house. When her husband (whose abuse prompted her to take the course) came home after drinking and playing poker with his buddies, he lunged

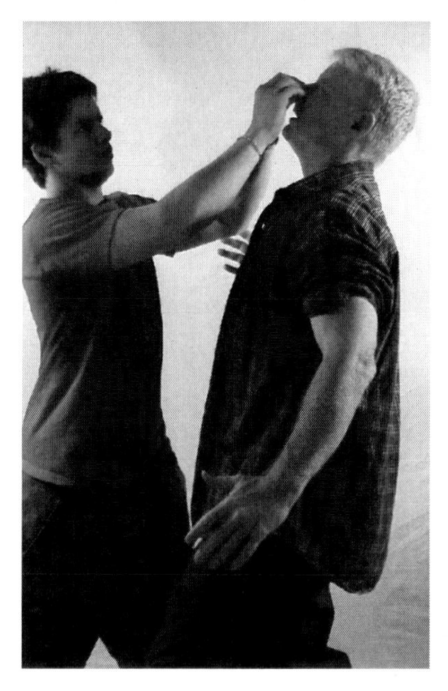

Strike to the eyes.

at her to vent his frustration over losing half his paycheck. In the past, she would have recoiled, frozen by fear, and taken the beating. This time she was resolved not to be a victim. She turned toward him and lunged at his eyes with both hands outstretched, yelling, "EYES!"

She never got closer than a foot away from his eyes, but her yell was so strong and her intent so clear that hubby reared back as if he had actually been struck in the eyes, hitting his head against the wall and knocking himself out cold. As a postscript, this woman ended up leaving her abusive relationship a month after the course was over, having experienced, as most graduates do, a newfound self-respect and realized that no one ever deserves to be treated abusively. I consider this a helluva great success story.

Nose and Jaw

The nose is another obvious good target. Anyone who has ever been popped even lightly on this bony protuberance knows the instant pain and tears this sensitive area produces. Break the nose, and the fight is usually over right there. The jaw is a harder spot to hit but well worth the effort when a good shot is delivered.

There is a myth that driving the nose upward into the brain can kill someone. Although anything is possible, experiments done on cadavers have shown that this is nearly impossible to accomplish. The cartilage in the nose is soft and resilient and will usually collapse before penetrating the brain in this manner. There reportedly is a complicated two-step process where brain penetration can be accomplished, but I choose not to go into that here. My point is that in a self-defense situation, hit the nose as hard as you can if it becomes available as a target. You will not cause death to the attacker by doing so, and it may well end the fight right there.

Throat

The throat is an excellent target because it is fairly accessible and cannot be strengthened to take a full-force strike. In a real situation, the throat makes a highly effective target. It can be struck in a number of ways to slow down and even finish an attacker if enough force is applied. We do not use strikes to the throat in FAST Defense because of the protective foam padding used on the bulletman helmet that covers the throat for safety reasons. This is one of the few limitations of the bulletman armor, and it is something we work around easily by emphasizing full-power eye, face, and head strikes. I have had overly aggressive students reach in under the helmet to grab my throat, and I can attest to the vulnerability of this spot.

Groin

The groin has received acclaim as the world's greatest target and also the world's worst. Many of our women students state that they were strongly conditioned never to hit a guy in the groin. My response to them is, "Who taught you that?" Typically, the answer is, "A guy!" But the negative connotations go beyond that. A while back I was speaking to a burly police officer who trains SWAT teams. He said he never teaches groin strikes to his civilian self-defense students. His reasoning was that when he and his fellow SWAT team guys spar, they purposely allow groin kicks and are never able to land them. Although this has merit in the context of sparring, in my experience it does not hold true in real-life self-defense situations. In sparring both participants are prepared for groin and other strikes. They are not in the full adrenal rush, and they are not succumbing to the debilitating effects of intense fear. I used to spar in the marines and in other martial arts classes, and we also would allow groin strikes. Like my SWAT friend, I never got tagged in the privates during such an athletic contest. But in street self-defense situations, I have successfully used front kicks to the groin to survive two separate gang attacks. In one I kicked the leader in the groin as he came at me and watched with amazement as this huge guy dropped like a building that had just been demolished. He even kicked up a cloud of dust on impact. In another I got into a standing clench with a guy who picked a fight with me. Grabbing my wrists to keep me from hitting him, my opponent stood squared off to me and unwittingly exposed his groin area. I popped him a quick one in the family jewels. People simply do not respond in real situations the way they might in classic training. It was the easiest thing in the world to bring my foot up into his groin, and he too dropped like a rock.

I want to be clear that I am not saying all fights will be this easy or that groin shots will just appear with blinking red lights and a sign saying, "Kick me!" But as a general rule, the groin is an accessible and highly effective target for any defender. Any guy will tell you it sucks a lot to be hit in the groin. And it doesn't take much force. At the age of 6 my son dropped me one day with a playful errant kick to my testicles. He stood there in amazement, wondering why Dad was writhing in pain on the ground. Enough said . . .

Ribs/Solar Plexus

Most body armor is padded well to allow the student to hit full-force to vulnerable areas on the torso such as the solar plexus and the ribs. Thus, most martial arts and self-defense systems focus on areas of the torso as full-force targets because the head and the groin are not adequately protected for the instructor. Back in my days of full-contact sparring, I sustained cracked ribs in training, and that was no fun at all! I also had the wind knocked out of me by a good shot to the solar plexus, which was no fun either. But I can't say that any of those strikes would have stopped a very determined attacker.

In my bulletman suit I receive good strikes to my torso from strong martial artists who routinely practice hitting these areas. Commonly these strikes feel like annoying little nuisances, even against bare skin. In the adrenal rush they are easy to deflect or even walk right through on the way to attack the student who just got knocked off balance by throwing the strike. I'm not saying that torso strikes won't work. Undoubtedly, there are folks out there who have knocked the wind out of their attacker and even broken ribs. But in my experience the torso targets do not represent the best assortment of consistent show stoppers. I view the torso as a nice place to visit on the way up or down to better targets.

Knees

The knees are definitely vulnerable areas on the body that, when hit, can cause a great deal of damage to the attacker. In fact, they are such good targets that no amount of protection has been found adequate for the padded attacker to endure full-force strikes to the knees from adrenalized students. This is one of the few real limitations of the bulletman body armor. Thus we don't encourage students to use strikes to the knees in class. Furthermore, even if we did, our own empirical evidence suggests that the knee may not be the most practical area to target under adrenal stress. Many of the students I come across are accomplished leg kickers, having practiced Muay Thai and other low-kick arts, and they commonly raise the question of what would happen if they were allowed to use these kicks that they are so well versed in against the bulletman in a fight scenario. So I have given a select few permission to kick me in the legs if the opportunity arose during one of our scenarios. I did so knowing that under a severe adrenal rush, the propensity is to go headhunting and focus on upper-body strikes and targets. (In my 35,000-plus fights in these classes, this has become evident over and over.) Sure enough, even these well-seasoned leg kickers often forgot all about targeting the knees or thighs and went straight to trying to punch my lights out (which they did quite well).

That said, we do instruct students to kick viciously to the knees if they should ever end up on the ground defending against a real-life attacker. We have had students report that they were knocked to the ground in street altercations after taking the course and very successfully dispatched their still-standing attackers with a good kick to the knee. This is because when you are on the ground the angle to the knee of a standing person is so clear and vulnerable. It is totally different when both people are standing; the angles don't work nearly as well, and the propensity is to go after the attacker's head as a target.

Feet/Instep

Many an attacker has been dissuaded by a good stomp to the foot or instep area. We used to teach this strike in our classes, but despite padding, bulletmen ended up with broken feet. One famous Model Mugging success story is that of a woman who was attacked after leaving her job as a cocktail waitress. Her Model Mugging training kicked in when some guy grabbed her from behind as she walked to her car. She stomped on his instep, driving her four-inch stiletto heel through his foot and into the asphalt parking lot. He screamed, let go of her, and fell backward, apparently hitting his head on the asphalt. Having lost the shoe that impaled her attacker, she took a couple of Cinderella-style hops before kicking off her other shoe and running to the bouncer, who came out and found the bad guy still unconscious. Since she had little memory of the attack (a common occurrence in real-life attacks), the account of the incident became clear only after the would-be attacker was interrogated in his hospital room.

While some targets typically work better than others, the bottom line is that hitting anywhere on an attacker with commitment and ferocity will have an effect. Again, you should always try to avoid a fight if at all possible. But if not, you must flip the switch and fight for all you are worth until you can either get away safely or stop the attacker. Since fighting is an absolute last resort, you are not going to throw a strike to any particular area and stand back to admire your handiwork. You must fight like a demon possessed and keep on fighting until the threat is eliminated.

Chapter 7

The Bulletman Armor

One of the biggest misconceptions about adrenal stress response training is that it's all about the protective suit the mock attacker wears. Although it is essential to the physical training, body armor is not critical to training someone to deal effectively with adrenaline and fear. In fact, the EZ Defense course that I developed for the National Association of Professional Martial Artitsts (NAPMA) requires no armored assailant. It utilizes simple, fun drills that definitely adrenalize the students and provide the desired effects. Even people who have experienced the bulletman suit speak very highly of the non-suited EZ Defense methodology. It bears repeating here that the awareness and verbal skills we teach are paramount in effective real-life self-defense, and these require no body armor to teach effectively. Still, there is no refuting that a program that uses adequate body armor provides more intense and thus more effective self-defense training.

There are literally dozens of protective suits on the market that are designed to protect the instructor to varying degrees so that students can hit with greater power than they could against someone who is not padded. In the mad rush to cash in on the self-defense industry and make a fast buck, more than a few suits have popped up on the market. I have worn virtually every suit out there and have some very strong opinions on the responsible use of padded assailant training. I urge extreme caution in selecting and using a protective suit for any type of training.

FAST Defense body armor.

My bulletman suit is a semicustomized 35-pound collaboration of body armor featuring a large, silver-domed helmet that protects the mock assailant's head against full-force strikes. To date I have logged well over 35,000 fights against students ranging from meek and mild grandmothers to martial arts masters and multilevel black belts the size of pro football defensive backs. I use this suit for a very good reason: it is simply the very best protection I have found for teaching adrenal stress response training.

The author built all of these helmets. Although they look like real bulletman helmets, they were inferior, and those who used them sustained injuries that wouldn't have happened if they had bought the real ones. (Photo by Moses Street.)

The bulletman suit is one of those things that people love to badmouth. It's been referred to as the Pillsbury Doughboy, the Michelin Man, the padded "dummy" (referring probably more to the guy inside than outside), and a slew of other equally demeaning and no less colorful descriptions. Because the helmet must be quite large to be able to absorb the full-force blows, some have denounced it as being unrealistic for the student. From someone who has not experienced the training, this is not an unfair assessment. The rational mind might look at this behemoth wrapped in duct tape and dismiss it in short order. The catch is that the rational mind is not functioning out there in the scenarios against the bulletman. Virtually everyone who has ever taken this training says that the scenario was as real as any fight they had ever been in and that the size of the helmet was not a factor at all in the adrenal rush. Afterward they are typically shaking and don't have a clear memory of the

The largest congregation of bulletmen ever at a FAST Defense instructors' retreat.

fight. I was amazed the first time I was attacked by a bulletman in a class. I had a total flashback to real experiences and afterward could not clearly remember what had happened.

I hear a lot from folks espousing this or that suit as really being able to take full-force blows, and I always try any such suit personally before making any criticism. Some of the commercially available protective suits are pretty well made, and others are pretty scary. The major problem is that often the designers and the end users are not in sync when it comes to the purposes and safe use of each particular suit. There is a big difference between symmetric and asymmetric training and the safety parameters within each respective category. A good example of this, in my opinion, is the RedMan suit. It was originally designed for police baton training. Such training is asymmetric, with the instructor playing a fully adrenalized attacker and the students responding with full-force strikes to the knees and abdomen with the baton as is authorized for law enforcement agents. The RedMan is a good suit for this type of scenario-based law-enforcement training, though it's a bit difficult to move in. The problem lies in martial artists buying this suit to teach self-defense to their students and the general public. This suit (and almost invariably all others) is not made to take full-force strikes to the head or groin. The manufacturer wisely places a disclaimer with each suit that says it is not designed to take strikes "hard enough to cause pain" or for virtually any strikes to the head or the groin area. Yet many a well-meaning instructor has seen a video of a FAST Defense, RMCAT, or Model Mugging class, bought this or another commercially available suit, and gotten a concussion or worse from allowing students to strike his head full force. This is an example of a suit designed for asymmetric training but not for full-force, empty-hand training.

Other suits are designed for symmetric training. Essentially, this is highly advanced sparring gear. The idea is to pad up both participants so they can practice their sparring and other techniques against each other. Although these suits are not designed for total full-force strikes to the head, someone with good skill, strength, and dexterity can move well and simulate a pretty extreme fight against a similarly suited and skilled person in the symmetric paradigm. However, when people have used these suits in asymmetric training against fully adrenalized defenders, many of them have sustained injuries to their heads and groin.

The bottom line is I have yet to find anything superior or even close to the protection of the bulletman suit for the training I do. Believe me, if I come across something better, I will be the first to use it and talk it up like crazy. When choosing the right body armor, it is important for instructors to assess the following:

What is the purpose for training in the suit (i.e., what is your intended outcome for the student—stand-up fighting, kicking and punching, grappling, ground fighting, joint manipulation, etc.)?

Are you planning to do asymmetric or symmetric training? What is the type of suit you wish to use really made for, and what are its parameters regarding mobility versus safety and its specific safe areas to strike?

Possible answers to these questions by an instructor of adrenal stress response training are as follows:

a. *I wish to teach full-force self-defense to martial artists and the general public.* I am not looking to train UFC fighters or professional ring fighters. My intention is to allow students to flip the switch and apply simple gross motor strikes to vulnerable areas on the attacker (specifically head and groin and all points in between). I will also be doing simple ground fighting using full-contact strikes, little or no joint manipulations, and weapons defense both standing and on the ground.

b. *I am planning to do asymmetric training.* Only the instructor will wear a suit (although the students may sometimes wear light headgear and wrist guards), and I will be playing out scenarios that fully adrenalize the students to simulate as real an attack as possible. I will not be using this suit to spar against another suited opponent.

c. *I need a suit that can withstand full-force strikes to the head and groin, as well as protect the torso and ribs and back area.* It needs to provide maximum protection, especially to my head and neck, yet still be mobile enough to be realistic. It has to be strong enough to withstand at least a few years of continued punishment.

As I said, I have tried every piece of gear that is commercially available in my never-ending pursuit of the very best protection possible. After 17 years of padded assailant training, I am not willing to compromise safety to cut costs. I tried making suits for my bulletman team back when I was too cheap to buy the right ones. I sustained five concussions from the first suit I made, and the other guys are still pissed at me for their own injuries and the years of chiropractic adjustments that these suits made necessary. For full-on adrenal stress response scenario-based self-defense training, I will only use the bulletman suit.

It is important to note that the bulletman body armor is not commercially available on a large scale to just anyone who wants it. You cannot buy one off the shelves of your local martial arts school or sporting goods store. Each suit is semicustomized for the wearer and requires specific fitting and training to ensure safety for instructor and student alike. I do not make or sell the bulletman armor. I simply provide the fitting and training for the suit.

THE SUIT IS NOT THE TECHNOLOGY

In the good ol' days, I was required to train on the West Coast for two weeks of 14-hour days in the suit, apprentice back home for three months with an established Model Mugging group, then train for another two weeks on the East Coast to finally get certified. Although I consider this a bit extreme, it was important to be fully qualified for the level of intensity that we were putting our students and ourselves through. Over the years I have been able to synthesize the training for students as well as instructors so that it is much more time-efficient. But the fact remains that even with the very best body armor, one must be trained correctly for the safety and efficacy of students and instructors alike. The teaching method is even more important than the particular body armor in scenario-based adrenal stress response training.

Chapter 8

Teaching Methodology: A Deeper Look

Adrenal stress response training employs state-of-the-art Olympic coaching and sports psychology concepts as well as martial arts training methods to teach students to create muscle memory quickly and efficiently. Even more importantly, this training literally reconditions old, ineffective knee-jerk responses to fear by replacing them with new, effective responses that allow people to respond quickly and appropriately in the heat of battle! People who used to freeze up under stress learn to fire up and respond should the need ever arise in real life. Conversely, those hotheads who have the tendency to lose control and go off at the slightest provocation learn how to dial themselves back and stay cool in the heat of the moment.

The FAST Defense teaching methodology I have developed over the years follows a very specific format, the details of which follow.

INTRODUCTIONS

We open with a short introduction to scenario-based adrenal stress response training methodology, followed by staff introductions. The students then share why they are taking the course and what goals they wish to achieve. This is the beginning of the group bonding that will come into play later.

AWARENESS DRILLS

Next we have the students form two lines facing each other to begin the interactive awareness drills. These are designed to create awareness of the different levels of threat and how to identify them, the specific cues predators typically look for in selecting potential victims, and the common mistakes people make under duress that can make them inviting victims.

BOUNDARY-SETTING SCENARIOS

Next comes the all-important verbal and physical boundary-setting portion of the course. This begins the formal scenario-based training against the woofers. The students line up single-file against a wall. The instructors explain the color code of verbal and physical defense and demonstrate a low-level verbal attack. This clearly portrays the intention of the exercise, which is for each student to experience a verbal-threat scenario and effectively employ proper body language, eye contact, and verbal skills to de-escalate the threat. Following the demonstration, each student comes out on the floor one at a time to do his or her specific scenario in front of the group. While this may sound like a very simple thing to do, in actuality it is the scariest part of the class for most people. On top of the stress of dealing with the woofer, students typically experience a good amount of performance anxiety during this drill. This is by design: it elicits a good adrenal rush and thereby lends a great deal of realism to the fear that they are training to overcome.

The woofer's job is to begin each verbal assault with normal conversation, or at yellow-alert level, and escalate the threat up to orange-alert level, where the student experiences a moderate adrenal rush and implements the appropriate defensive strategies. Throughout the scenario, a female instructor (the coach) is right behind the student to help him or her fix any mistakes or problems that arise. If the student falters, the woofer and coach work together skillfully to guide the student through any blocks to a successful defense. The coach's voice and direction play a critical role in dynamically guiding the student and helping to smooth out any rough spots he or she may encounter. This circumvents the need to stop in the middle of the scenario when a mistake occurs.

Meanwhile, the rest of the students watch intently from the line to observe and learn from each scenario. Once the student makes a credible stand by taking a good orange-alert-level stance and using proper eye contact and verbal skills, the woofer rewards the student by backing off. That student then goes to the end of line while the rest of the students cheer, bringing that student back into the group and launching the next person into his or her scenario.

When all of the students have completed their first scenario, the process is repeated. This time the woofer increases the intensity of the threat to the red-alert level. These scenarios get very heated, and there is a good deal of cussing and innuendo as the woofer tries to push the student's buttons. Typically the students do very well with this despite the increased intensity because it is their second time through and they have already developed a degree of desensitization to the woof. Once again, as soon as each student employs the correct red-alert-level defensive techniques, the woofer backs off. Once all the students have completed their two verbal scenarios, the instructors conduct a debriefing before moving on to the next module.

The goal of the awareness and boundary-setting modules is to equip the students with the skills to prevent most conflicts from becoming physical. Once again, this is the best self-defense of all, because once an altercation does become physical, not only must you win the actual fight, but you might also have to win again when your attacker returns days later with a gun or with five buddies, or when you wind up in court on assault charges. Crazy as it seems, there are legal precedents wherein a defender has injured an attacker and then the attacker has sued the victim for assault and prevailed. However, in those cases where the awareness and boundary-setting techniques fail to thwart an attack, physical techniques are the only option. Learning and practicing those techniques is the next step of FAST Defense instruction.

PHYSICAL TECHNIQUE DRILLS AND SCENARIOS

Since people can only access about five bits of information during an adrenal fear rush, it follows they can apply about five techniques in real self-defense—*if* they are trained to react correctly in the adrenal rush. The five techniques we use in FAST Defense are all gross motor skills and very easy for almost anyone to apply, regardless of physical dexterity or strength. They are 1) palm-heel strikes, 2) strikes to the eyes, 3) elbow strikes, 4) knee strikes, and 5) slaps to the groin—for rear bear hug attacks.

The adrenal stress response training I originally received used an ingenious step-by-step methodology to help students attain a high level of physical dexterity very quickly. It did not take me months or years to master the movements; the method was based on adrenalizing students in incremental degrees while engineering a successful reaction using simple physical skills. I have further modified this regimen to create the dynamic teaching methodology I use today to consistently train students to rather astounding levels of physical skill and power in a very short amount of time.

Step One

In FAST Defense we begin by teaching the techniques in slow-motion, rhythmic patterns while the students say each technique aloud. Each of the five techniques is practiced with highly exaggerated movement and no speed or power. The main idea is to get students to emphasize the use of their hips. When adrenalized, most people lock up their hips, which manifests as upper-body flailing. The use of the voice is important here because it conditions the students to breathe from the very start of the training. Particularly for martial artists, who are accustomed to training fast and hard, it is imperative to slow down and forget about the details of correct stance, traditional chambering, and so on. They find this difficult and often resist it because it is so foreign to their training. Many of them think I'm crazy when I teach this method, assuming the movements, being so large and slow, would never work in a real battle. I tell them that while I may well be crazy, right now they are not engaged in a fight but a learning process designed to maximize their power later when they get to that stage. So for now, I explain, the best thing they can do is slow down and make their movements as large and gross motor as possible because everything speeds up and shortens under duress.

Once the students have learned and practiced the five individual techniques a few times, they combine them into three different sequences that further ingrain these techniques into the muscle memory through the use of rhythm and repetition. It is important to point out that these sequences should be thought of as training wheels. Combinations are irrelevant in a real fight because you never know whether a particular strike will work or not. Thus, attempting to access and execute some preassigned combination or sequence conditioned in the high-road brain (difficult to impossible in the heat of battle anyway) could actually work against you. Should any part of that combination fail to work, you could miss crucial targets that present themselves in the unpredictable course of combat as you focus on the goal of getting that next predetermined strike in. A fight is as simple as looking for a target and hitting it as hard as possible.

That said, the training sequences we use in FAST Defense do act as great learning vehicles by enabling students to practice the strikes as a series in a rhythmic, flowing manner. Modern-day Olympic coaches use this same methodology to provide athletes with muscle memory in a very short amount of time without the need for thousands of repetitions. Furthermore, because the training sequences are conditioned in the low-road brain, they are accessible under adrenal stress, so when the actual fights against the bulletman (or real attacker) occur, the defender is able to quickly access the appropriate strikes and deliver them full-force in whatever sequence will work to whatever targets are available.

Half-Count Coaching and Rhythm

While teaching these sequences, I have the group work in unison. Doing so helps slow down the fast students, speeds up the slower students, and also allows me to use the tempo of my voice to coordinate the group. Over time, this voice coaching technique, which I call half-count coaching, has proven invaluable to taking a group with varying abilities through the process in a very short amount of time. If you think in terms of rhythm, every strike being delivered is on a one count, and on the half count (the space between each strike) I simply tell students the next strike they will do. There are three major benefits to this:

1) Through half-count coaching the instructor can set a good rhythm and tempo for the group. By telling the students what they will do next, the instructor minimizes the amount of thinking they actually must do so they can focus on doing the techniques exactly as prescribed, in slow, exaggerated movements. By not thinking, they can feel the movements better as they get out of their self-critical minds and into their bodies.

2) Half-count coaching, correctly applied, sets a rhythm that literally changes brain patterns and promotes relaxation. It facilitates activity in the low-road brain, the part that will be functioning in a real-life assault. After years of working with many thousands of students, I have come to the solid conclusion that we humans are typically our own worst enemies when it comes to learning physical skills. Physical movement

is best learned and applied by the body, not the self-aware mind. Take, for example, a good dancer who creates wonderful physical expression through rhythm and flow. This cannot be accomplished through the thinking mind. We've all seen people on the dance floor who try to think their way through the dance (or perhaps we've been that person ourselves). It is the same with self-defense movements. In the fight-or-flight response, the conscious, self-critical mind, the high-road brain, shuts down, and the movements must come naturally and immediately to work at all. There is no better or quicker way to train this than through rhythmic teaching.

3) Half-count coaching reduces mistakes and permits easy correction for the instructor. With the group working as one rhythmic, cohesive unit, the instructor can easily recognize and correct mistakes without stopping to point out who made what mistake. Often when working with a martial arts group, the instructors will naturally attach to a student who is having trouble. In my experience this is disruptive and actually slows down the learning process. Students who are having trouble will typically be extremely self-conscious and self-aware (in other words, *way* up in their heads). Singling them out will usually make them even more self-conscious and nervous, exacerbating the situation. I prefer to address the group as a whole, telling them that if they get out of sync with the group they should just fake it and make every effort to get back in sync as soon as possible. I also assure them that in a real fight the attacker doesn't care if you get out of sequence and do something slightly wrong. The worst thing you can do in a fight

is stop and judge yourself harshly for making a mistake (which would be ludicrous when defending yourself); yet that is exactly what many students do in the learning process. Since people will do what they have trained to do, they benefit more from continuing through with the sequence by faking it if need be. I then simply have the entire class repeat the sequence together again, providing a little extra half-count coaching to everyone in order to help those who are having trouble through their blocks. It never takes more than four to five repetitions of each of the three sequences to get the whole group moving like a finely tuned machine.

Step Two

The next phase marks the beginning of the group dynamics that will be used for the duration of the course. First the students are asked to line up against a wall, facing the center of the room. One at a time they come out and practice the first sequence with a male instructor who is holding a standard martial arts shield. The intention is to reinforce the slow-motion, exaggerated movements in order to maximize power and minimize flailing later when they fight against the bulletmen. The very act of performing in front of their fellow students elicits an adrenal rush. Again, this is by design and is part of the process of desensitizing each student to the adrenal rush one small increment at a time. The coach is always present to provide the half-count coaching and virtually think for the student as necessary.

You may be thinking that this is unrealistic training because there won't be any coach present in a real altercation. But in a sense, he or she will be. Over the years we have had many students recount subconsciously hearing the voice of their coach in real-life altercations years after taking the course. The power of this training is that it effectively conditions the subconscious part of the brain that is functioning under duress.

Soft-Shield Technique

Using the same slow-motion, rhythmic manner practiced earlier with the entire class, the students practice the first sequence while the instructor with the shield provides the target. This is most effective when the shield holder also moves rhythmically to help keep the student slow and deliberate. I call this the soft-shield technique. Most martial artists hold the shield tightly and offer a lot of resistance in training. This results in short, constricted strikes that actually work against the defender when everything shortens up under adrenal stress. In the soft-shield technique it is held with little resistance to allow a full range of motion for each technique. This results in powerful full-range-of-motion strikes both in training and under the adrenal stress of a real attack.

Meanwhile, the students standing in line are strongly encouraged to take a powerful stance, move rhythmically, focus on the student out on the mat, and say the techniques along with him or her. This provides for a great deal of extra repetition for everyone and saves time overall. As instructors, we constantly reinforce the fact that much of adrenal stress response training takes place in the line. By mimicking the student on the floor, saying the techniques, and visualizing being that student, the other students get the benefit of doing the scenario many times, even though they will actually only do each scenario once individually at each stage of the training.

Once each student has practiced the first sequence individually with an instructor while the rest of the line actively watches, the class moves on to the second sequence to repeat the slow-motion process and then begins the third and final sequence.

Step Three

In this step we repeat what was done in step two but allow each student to hit the shield full force. It's important that the student stay present and focused by not yet getting fully adrenalized. This is easier said than done and requires some finesse on the instructor's part to accomplish, but it is important to the teaching process. Since the tendency is to shorten up the hip motion and hold the breath when fully adrenalized, both of which dramatically reduce power, the challenge at this stage is to keep the student slowed down in between strikes to condition maximum-power muscle memory. The student is reminded that this stage is about conditioning muscle memory to hit full force and that it is not yet an actual fight. Time and time again, I have observed that the students who can continue large, exaggerated strikes at this stage will hit very hard in the real fights when body motion is naturally shortening and speeding up. Conversely, those who speed up too much at this stage might flail and even freeze when the adrenaline rush hits.

At this stage the instructor uses the soft shield to facilitate full-force strikes without injury to the students. He is also in a position to see if students are holding their breath and to remind them to say the techniques, or at least exhale forcefully, on impact. Holding the breath is one of the most common and debilitating mistakes people make under duress. If students hold their breath at this stage, they will certainly do so in the fully adrenalized fights, at the expense of a great deal of power.

Once again, the entire class comes out on the floor one at a time for each of the three sequences while their classmates actively watch from the line.

Step Four

In this final step of the training process, the bulletmen don their protective gear and prepare to do battle. The students are once again lined up. I like to arrange the line so that stronger students are intermingled with weaker ones. It helps to have a somewhat balanced group so you don't get pockets of robust students followed by pockets of weaker students. I also like to start the scenarios with a strong student to set the tempo and finish with a strong student as an exclamation point.

As in the boundary-setting scenarios, each student comes out on the floor one at time in front of all their classmates. In the FAST Defense Basics course the fights are divided into standing attacks from the front and the rear. The coach instructs the student to close his or her eyes to add an element of surprise in terms of how and when the bulletman will attack. This also serves to escalate the adrenal rush.

The scenario begins when the bulletman either grabs or strikes the student or launches into a loud verbal assault. The line is encouraged to yell out the strikes and targets they see available so that they process the scenario as if they were actually fighting. This provides a great deal of extra practice for everyone as well as elevating the level of energy in the room. Not only does this "passive participation" help the students in the line learn, but it also helps the student in the actual fight. Just as the coach's verbal commands are conditioned into the subconscious minds of all of the students, so too is the cheering of their classmates. (Graduates of our programs have reported hearing their classmates' cheers when attacked in real life, stating that the cheering helped them overcome the fear/freeze response and fired them up to the same level of intensity they achieved back in their class.) The student then fights with all he or she has got until the bulletman is down in a "dead bug" protective position, indicating that he has taken at least a few solid knockout strikes. The coach loudly blows the whistle to stop the fight and help break the student out of the adrenal rush.

It is up to the male instructor to determine how much intensity he will give to each student to customize the experience for maximum effect. Too little and the student will not be challenged; too much will overload the student and defeat the purpose of fostering a successful experience. The objective is to have a fully adrenalized student focusing all of the emotional and biochemical power of the adrenal rush into full-force strikes to vulnerable areas on the attacker's body. In the suit, the padded instructor is fighting back with gusto and responding like a real attacker would. A good bulletman can elicit the adrenaline response in a heartbeat and literally coach the student through the fight by responding to good strikes and not responding to marginal or weak ones. It works with amazing consistency.

The concept is quite simple. Just as people can be conditioned to be victims (sometimes for a lifetime) in a single assault where they freeze up, they can also be reconditioned to replace that ineffectual response with a successful one that enables them to take action. Through scenario-based adrenal stress response training, the fear that causes most people to freeze or flail becomes their greatest ally. This reconditioning process can be achieved in as little as three hours of training and can literally last a lifetime. And while students have successfully defended themselves years after taking a half-day course without any further practice or refresher course, more is definitely better. We strongly encourage students to attend refresher and advanced courses. Each scenario a student experiences in FAST Defense exponentially increases the ability to deal with the adrenal rush and enhances self-defense skills.

The Sweet Spot

Whether in golf, tennis, horseback riding, self-defense, or any other physical undertaking, the ultimate goal is to find the "sweet spot," that Zen-like state that occurs when you get out of the head and totally into the body. To counter the risk of getting too philosophical here, the sweet spot in self-defense is found in that totally focused strike where the body, mind, and spirit suddenly merge to knock the attacker senseless. The goal of the four-step teaching methodology is to prepare the student to find this sweet spot. The job of the bulletman is to dynamically coach the student to find these sweet spots in the heat of battle. The bulletman will not end any scenario until the student delivers at least three seriously powerful blows that would stop just about any assailant. If the student is not finding his or her power (usually due to flailing induced by fear), the bulletman has to react realistically by cranking up the intensity and forcing the student to break through his or her barriers. When this is done skillfully, the students literally burst out of their bubbles and strike with a ferocity that can be surprising. In this mode, the bulletman needs to allow each student to get full-force power programmed into muscle memory. Sometimes he will have to sustain shots that would drop a real attacker and continue fighting, just to provide that sweet-spot shot to the student. Once this muscle memory exists, the students find their bodies literally searching out the sweet spot in subsequent scenarios. With practice, they become capable of dealing effectively with very difficult scenarios and are able to find a plethora of sweet-spot strikes in the craziness of the battle.

For a time, my Colorado bulletman team would suit up and fight each other to explore how far we could take this sweet-spot idea. We had all developed certain techniques that we preferred over others, dictated by our particular size, strength, and agility levels. My personal favorite is the forward elbow (forearm) strike to the head or throat, a powerhouse blow that is usually very difficult for most people to land because it requires a total commitment to enter and deliver. After three such sessions, I was hitting so hard that one of our bulletmen was cross-eyed for a couple of days after I delivered an elbow to his head. I'm not telling you this to impress you (it actually scared the hell out of us, and we stopped these training sessions as a result) but to give you an idea of the potential of this training.

VIDEO DEBRIEFING

After the fights are completed, the students take a short break before the final video review of the fights. This is an important facet of the training because most of the students will have little recollection of what they actually did in their fights as a result of the critical stress amnesia that occurs during the adrenal rush. Viewing the video of their fights provides their conscious minds with the visual confirmation that they really did fight with all the heart and spirit that we consistently see our students achieve.

In each video debriefing I encourage the students not to focus on the strikes they missed but on the ones that really landed. By focusing on the sweet spots they had and visualizing them, they train their minds and bodies to seek out these same strikes in later scenarios. Students who come back for refresher and advanced classes demonstrate amazing abilities to find vulnerable areas on the attacker and deliver sweet-spot shots, even when the bulletmen know exactly what the students are going to do and try to avoid it.

I used to offer monthly Friday night refresher courses for our Denver-area graduates. One group came for three months straight and got so powerful they were injuring our best bulletmen. It became quite clear that they could defend themselves very well and needed no more training. I told them they should go enjoy their Friday evenings elsewhere! These students had found the sweet spot.

This experience directly counters the idea that thousands of repetitions are needed to create muscle memory. It has proved to us that it can take as few as three or four fights for a student to develop the ability to respond instantly with remarkable speed and power.

CLOSING CIRCLE

The final phase of the instruction is the closing circle, where we allow the students to debrief by relating their personal subjective experience of the course. They each have a turn to discuss whether they obtained their goals for the course and share whatever lessons and observations stand out in their minds at that particular moment. It is amazing how much information surfaces during this debriefing, as listening to each other serves to draw out even more from the students—thoughts and responses that might otherwise remain buried in the subconscious.

After 17 years of sitting in untold numbers of these closing circles, I still have not had even one person be less than totally impressed with this teaching process. It is a real challenge for us to convey the full power of this training or for anyone to comprehend it without experiencing it firsthand. But my experience in these debriefing sessions has confirmed for me that virtually everyone who does experience it loves it!

CUSTOM SCENARIOS—POWERFUL MOJO

The psychological breakthroughs that commonly occur in this type of training are what have kept me doing this work long beyond what someone with any sense would do. As a result, I have been able to take the art of the bulletman to profound levels. Before each scenario I find that I can now calm my mind and allow my intuition to feed me information to make the scenario as realistic as possible. Sometimes things happen that border on the surreal.

During our weekend intensives, we allow the students to recreate a worst fear or a situation that has actually occurred to them in the past. I have had numerous students come up after a particular scenario where I was really tuned into my role and say things like, "How did you know to say what my uncle said to me before he raped me when I was 7?" Another young woman said that during her scenario she smelled the cigar her kidnapper was smoking while he held her captive for five hours and raped her multiple times.

Perhaps the most powerful and heart-wrenching experience for me in the suit occurred when I had to play out the same crazed killer character in three separate classes. The first time, a woman came to us to work through a horrible incident that had happened to the family of her best friend in the next town over. A teenage boy had spent the evening sitting for a young boy at the home of a family friend. Later that night, after having been dropped off at home by the boy's father, the teenager returned to the house where he had babysat earlier and killed the father and son with a hammer.

The story was well publicized and obviously had a devastating effect on the entire community, including my staff and me. This woman chose to replay the scenario in a way that gave her the opportunity to arrive and save the boy, whom she knew very well. This was sanctioned by her therapist for the therapeutic benefit that these custom scenarios had proven to provide. I was very motivated to help this woman heal from her incredible pain. It took on even deeper significance for me because at the time my son was about the same age as the boy who had been killed.

I calmed myself to really allow the essence of the situation into my mind and body, wanting with all my heart to make it as realistic as I could so that this woman could experience the breakthrough she so desperately needed. I could almost feel the spirit of that teenage murderer enter me as I played out going after the young boy so she could rescue him and dispatch me. Never had I experienced the fury she unleashed as she transformed all of her untapped pain and heartache into unimaginable power. She made short work of dispatching me, and the next thing I knew I was flat on my back looking up into her face as she sent an unearthly howl of unfathomable remorse and release down into my supine form. A flood of almost visible toxic sludge was pouring out of her into me. And then it was over as the students gathered around her exhausted form.

It took a moment for me to regain my body and conscious mind. Suddenly, my self-aware mind was flooded with waves of emotion as I tried to assimilate what had happened. If such a thing as a possession can exist, it did in me that day. I don't remember how I got there, but in a flash I was outside the building crying uncontrollably, frantically beating my heavily padded helmeted head against a brick wall to exorcise the demon that threatened to take control. After some minutes I regained myself and returned to the room, where I had to continue the class. It took me days to fully recover from this. But it wasn't over yet.

Author in his bulletman armor.

Months later, yearning for a similar breakthrough, the sister of the murdered boy came through the course on the advice of her friend and her therapist. Once again I had to play out the same scenario. Because I had already played this character and wanted so badly to help this tormented woman, I fell into the role even deeper than before. Once again the student had an earth-shattering breakthrough. Again the toxic sludge poured into me as she too let out a primal scream of utter release. And once again I was suddenly outside slamming the demons out of me against the wall. But my job was still not done.

About a year later, the mother came through the course. She was the sweetest woman one could imagine, yet the cloud that hung over her was palpable. The entire class was moved to the core with empathy as she slowly opened up over the weekend and told her story. Finally, it was custom scenario time. My fellow bulletman offered to do the scenario for me, God bless him. But this was something I had to do, having come this far. Who else could do it as I had the opportunity to do? Besides, I knew what I was in for, and it was something I wouldn't have asked anyone else to do.

Never had I wanted to help someone so much as I did this lovely soul. Into the abyss we went, and I quickly lost any conscious awareness of what was happening. All I know is that we joined arms and dove into the depths of hell—and my job was to be the platform from which she would leap back out to rediscover the joy of life that had so long escaped her. It seemed an eternity before I was on the ground, which seemed to shake beneath my stunned form. This time as she looked down at me, the murderer's face painted in her mind upon my helmet, I willed the toxic sludge to leave her body forever and flow into me. Somehow I was aware of a force of love—call it God, call it what you will—that was manifesting in the incredible power of those life-changing moments. I again found myself outside becoming one with the brick wall. But this time was different. Afterward I felt almost transparent, like the sins of the world had washed into and through me, leaving me in an altered state that is impossible to explain.

I do remember walking back into the room where the group was still in a protective circle around this woman, a warrior of epic proportions. My female coach saw me enter, and the circle magically opened, allowing me and this reborn woman to embrace. It was an incredibly emotional moment for everyone present. Her beautiful boy was irrevocably snatched from this life. But that day the world changed—for her, for her family, and for me. And being part of it will forever touch my heart.

Chapter 9

The FAST Defense Instructor Team

Although simple in concept, teaching FAST Defense training is not so simple in practice. It takes a well-trained team of instructors to produce consistent results, and it requires a great deal of care and validation of students' fears to get them through this process. Scenario-based adrenal stress response training has the power to bring about great healing and develop very effective self-defense prowess. Unfortunately, it also has the power to do great harm. Because of the realism of the scenarios, students can actually be traumatized if skill and caution are not used, As such, instructors need to be well trained and acutely aware of their own personal issues so that they can deal with the intense emotions that will inevitably arise.

A large percentage of our students have previously experienced some sort of victimization. The FBI reports that one in three women will be sexually assaulted in her lifetime. Factor in the sexual harassment, verbal innuendos, and other intimidation that women are bombarded with regularly in our society, and you will appreciate why these women are already on edge. Any display of macho attitude will shut them down and make the teaching process difficult if not completely ineffective.

Our focus is always on making our students feel safe and, by respecting their vulnerability, facilitating their trust in us as instructors. As a result, our female students learn better and enjoy the process. Our male students experience a similar result. Since few men have ever learned to defend themselves adequately, this process is very rewarding. When done correctly, it enables students to transform their fears into power and achieve remarkable gains in their self-confidence and defensibility.

Although any qualified instructor, regardless of gender, can potentially teach FAST Defense, it is preferable to have at least two male instructors and one female instructor, as well as one or more assistants, per course. The success of the verbal boundary-setting drills lies in creating a simulated scenario that is believable to your student. Due to sociological conditioning, most students will more readily associate danger with a male versus a female assailant. However, because of the graphic nature of the verbal drills, it is calming to the students to have a strong female instructor by their side coaching them. The use of both a male and female instructor is also important when demonstrating the kinds of physical boundary situations female students could potentially face so that they can get a visual example of how a woman can effectively back down a man. Many students also benefit from seeing behaviors they may never have associated with a particular gender, such as empathetic and caring behavior from the male instructor or strong, assertive behaviors from the female instructor.

WOOFER

For scenario-based training to work, there must be someone to play the role of a credible bad guy. We call this guy the woofer. Just like a dog trying to intimidate its victim by going "woof woof," the woofer's objective is to elicit an adrenal response in the student through a barrage of verbal assaults, foul language, and innuendo. Although woofing can look simple, like some guy talking a bunch of trash, it's actually a very refined art that requires a great deal of sensitivity and skill. We can't go bringing in some ex-con to play the woofer just because he has woofed it up a lot in real life. Woofing is a back-and-forth chess game between woofer and student. Although it usually creates a very powerful experience for the student when done correctly, it can also do harm if done poorly.

I travel full time, training instructor teams of woofers and coaches. It is beyond the scope of a book to convey this methodology in detail. But here are some basic woofing tips that are standard in woofer training:

- *Start out with just a simple disguise and a few basic characters of woofers.* Some examples are a drunken panhandler, an obnoxious construction worker, a stalker, or an aggressive coworker.

- *Always let the student win.* Woofing is a chess game of give and take, not just a barrage of obscenities.

- *Stay at least two arm's lengths away from the student.* New woofers have a tendency to move in too close, replacing intensity with proximity. If the woofer gets in too close, it might be appropriate for the student to strike, which is not the intention of this drill.

- *Back off or respond in some other way to reward the student when he or she does it correctly.* Since the verbal scenarios are the hardest ones for the students to perform in scenario-based training, you do not want to frustrate and discourage them by overdoing it.

- *Start out simply and practice with friends to allow yourself to learn this very unique craft.* Over time you will become very fluid with your woofing and "ad-lib" each scenario like an actor does on stage.

Playing the woofer.

Many martial arts school owners and instructors worry that they will lose the respect of their students if seen as the woofer. This is understandable, yet what we find is that in the context of the program, the students not only understand why their instructors are doing this, but they also respect them for taking on these difficult roles to help others. Even so, it is important to wear a rudimentary disguise to distinguish the bad-guy woofer from the nice-guy instructor. This is easily done by making some simple changes in clothing, such as a hat and sunglasses.

The impact that woofing has to intimidate and even control people is amazing, and assailants know this and use it to their great advantage. In scenario-based adrenal stress response training, the woofer provides a tremendous service to students in first helping to desensitize them to the woof and then teaching them to overcome it by turning the woof on the woofer.

COACH

The role of the coach is the most difficult and important one in scenario-based training. Essentially, the coach runs the show. Each time the woofer engages a student in a scenario, the coach is there as a guardian angel standing over the student's shoulder, thinking and problem-solving for the student should his or her mind go blank. The coach initiates and finishes each and every scenario, plus arranges and watches over the line, making sure that all are involved and energetic. Should emotional meltdowns occur (and they will if the training is done correctly), it is the job of the coach to handle them and facilitate breakthroughs for the students as they relive old traumas or fears. The coach is there to steer the boat and also be the students' confidante in times of trouble.

Although men can make good coaches, ideally the coach should be a woman, especially when working with female students. A good female coach is extremely difficult to come by. This woman must exhibit a rare combination of qualities: empowered and confident, yet very empathetic and tuned in to the emotional and physical processes of her students. In addition, it is the coach's job to demonstrate every technique and every scenario that the students will be asked to do. She is also responsible for making sure everything goes safely amidst the chaos of the very realistic and fully adrenalized scenarios.

A coach at work, planting subconscious cues into the student's low-road brain during the scenario.

Being a coach is both exhausting and emotional, yet it is one of the most rewarding jobs of the instructor team. Coaches invariably feel the emotional pain the students experience as they battle their biggest inner demons. Yet they must remain unshaken and completely focused on the scenarios to assist the students in any way necessary. Scenario-based training is complex, and it takes a very sharp and experienced coach to handle the many facets of this powerful, transformational journey. A good coach is a friend, a mentor, and a miracle worker in one.

BULLETMEN

The instructor team is the vehicle that leads the students through the often-emotional roller coaster of adrenal stress response training. Integral to this team are the guys who have to be there as caring teachers on the one hand, yet realistically portray the character and demeanor of real-life predators and attackers on the other. It is vitally important that the students see the male instructors as caring human beings. The men who sign up for this work are pure gold. Psychological problems can manifest for the bulletmen if care is not taken to offset the negative impact of taking on these roles for the welfare of the students. Unfortunately, many of us learned this the hard way back in the pioneering days of this work.

At the time of my instructor training, this technology was 15 years old and was experiencing a renaissance as a powerful instrument of the feminist movement that was very alive in the late '80s. Back then the courses were only taught to women, due to the fear that teaching men might produce the next generation of "super-muggers." Of course, this fear-based mode of thinking was way off the mark. In truth, this course empowers people to take control of their lives at a very deep level. People who are thus empowered do not victimize others. Men who take the course actually leave with a softer demeanor as they replace old macho defenses with true confidence that belies the need to present that tough-guy image.

Author as a young "mugger."

Back then, we male instructor candidates had to pass psychological screening designed to determine that we weren't psychos who simply wanted to get our jollies by playing the muggers and rapists in these courses. Although this seemed necessary and prudent at the time, we eventually realized that only nice, caring guys are willing to jump through the many hoops necessary to get in these suits and play out these nasty roles for relatively little money. It was the yearning to help others and the stark reality that many of us had experienced some sort of abuse in the past ourselves that motivated us to undertake the profound physical and emotional journey required of male instructors.

Unfortunately, the intense focus on safety of the students overshadowed the need for emotional safety for the male instructors. Back then, a female instructor would teach the students the techniques with minimal male presence. We guys would essentially be marched out in our protective suits when it was time for the students to fight. We would elicit the students' adrenal fear rush (fancy terms for "scare the hell out of them") by playing the roles of various attackers. It was our job to make each scenario real enough for the student to experience an intense adrenal fear rush and allow her to transform that energy into full-force, emotionally charged strikes to our bodies. In effect, we were dredging up years or even decades of negative energy from deep within our students. Through this ingenious step-by-step process, the students learned to "flip the switch," break the freeze response, and turn all that energy into amazing power. Our job was to facilitate this transformation by drawing the negative out of the students and into us.

Once the fights were over, the male instructors were ushered out again, while the women proceeded to process the experience. We were left to ourselves to deal with the toxic sludge that was stuck inside our minds and bodies after the fights. Because we were seen only as the "bad guys" and never as the caring men that we were, and because we did not have the opportunity to express and process the inevitable conflicting emotions we felt, this toxicity remained within us. We were just nice guys trying to help women, and we simply didn't know what to do with these conflicting emotions. So we did the typical human thing and stuffed away those feelings to the deep, dark recesses of our psyches. With each successive class this toxic sludge-pile grew in us. Many of us started drinking or using drugs to dampen the emotional pain. When the emotional distress became too much for one very bighearted but severely depressed guy in a California chapter, he committed suicide.

Finally, we got some professional help and endeavored to rectify the problem. Now in this training we go to great lengths to have the men share the entire process with the students, giving us the opportunity to be seen as the caring men we are and, when appropriate, even share our own fears and feelings. This strategy has paid huge dividends for instructors and students alike, and it has reinforced the theory that a skilled team of female and male instructors should teach even all-female classes.

TRANSFERENCE AND COUNTERTRANSFERENCE

No discussion of this teaching methodology would be complete without a glimpse into the powerful dynamics of transference and countertransference. Transference is a normal and useful dynamic that occurs between teacher and student. In short, it is a trust that is developed by an instructor to get the student to respect and follow instruction. Although not necessary in a learning environment, it certainly helps when it is used constructively. Trust is a major factor in any learning relationship and facilitates a more lively and fun interaction between all parties. Transference happens all the time, and sometimes it results in students developing innocent crushes that most teachers aren't even aware of. The problem occurs when transference is allowed to go further than simple, healthy trust or an innocent crush.

Teachers and students alike have forever struggled with the dynamics of developing relationships with one another. This is simply human nature. But the reality is that in many cases where the parties have chosen to follow their hearts, the resultant romantic relationships have ended badly. Students who may be insecure or vulnerable often project unrealistic pictures onto their instructors in an effort to find something that's missing in their lives. A classic cinematic example is portrayed in the movie *Indiana Jones*. Jones, played by Harrison Ford, was a charismatic professor of archaeology who had the young women in his classroom all a-flutter. One admiring student wrote "I love you" on her eyelids, which caught Jones' shocked attention when she batted her eyes. Ford was playing a teacher who was simply passionate about his work and loved to teach; he wasn't some lecherous predator looking for young girls to prey on.

Although this was just a movie, the dynamic is very real in learning situations all over the world. Another good example of this occurs in the movie industry when actors come together for a short but intense journey while shooting a film. Many of these actors are playing roles with similar dynamics to those of the student-teacher relationship. Even seasoned actors fall prey to this powerful projection. Stories abound of quick Hollywood flings that destroy marriages and then die before the divorce papers are ever served.

Countertransference is where the instructor falls for the student, projecting his/her own desires and needs onto the person he/she has been entrusted to educate. As the relationship between teacher and student progresses, the opportunity for romantic fantasies becomes stronger. Most good instructors experience a softening and deeper caring for their students if they are doing their jobs correctly. But when the feelings go deeper than this, some very real difficulties can potentially arise should the instructors cross the line and betray the trust placed in them to care for their students. The discerning teacher or facilitator can identify and deal with these feelings before acting on them. The ones who cannot deal with these feelings responsibly often end up in tough situations. Sometimes such a relationship can work out, but much more often it has proven to be injurious to the involved parties.

Because the dynamics of FAST Defense are so emotionally intense, the potential for transference/countertransference is even greater than in a typical learning environment. Although there are a multitude of reasons for taking our courses, many students do so because they feel vulnerable. The process of uncovering and overcoming their fears can be powerful and dramatic.

Many students unprepared for such radical transformation are unable to digest and own their newfound sense of inner strength. Although in truth it was they who did the work to discard old traumas and take charge of their lives, some project a hero image onto the instructors for producing this change in them. Again, the discerning instructor will reflect this back onto the student by clearly stating that the work was and had to be done by the student. Our job as instructors is merely to point the way; the students have to make the journey themselves.

Sometimes no matter what we instructors say, the emotions are too strong to allow the student to discriminate, and the projection takes control. Many instructors have had adoring students call, write letters, send pictures, and even show up at their doors after finishing the course. It can be very intoxicating for instructors to have this happen, especially if they are under the spell of countertransference, because the truth is, seeing first-hand a person uncovering old layers of fear and opening like a rose is a beautiful thing. I have seen hundreds of students walk through the doors of the classroom hunched over, sunken-eyed, and bereft of any visible sense of spirit. And I have seen these same students undergo dramatic physical and emotional changes—literally becoming more beautiful before the instructors' and fellow students' eyes.

So powerful is the transference that can occur on both sides of the classroom that many relationships occurred in the early Model Mugging days of adrenal response training. These almost invariably turned sour because they were built on false projections on both sides. The student was the vulnerable princess waiting to be rescued and the instructor the dashing prince coming to the rescue. Back in the days when the female instructor was the primary teacher, many of the female students developed crushes on her for the same reasons.

Again, this dynamic occurs to varying degrees in any teaching environment, and people who get caught in the trap often leave good marriages for a fantasy that is doomed from the start. Many Model Mugging, Impact, and FAST Defense programs have adopted a six-month no-dating policy between staff and students. This rule is prudent because it permits time for the transference to pass and reality to set back in. Such a rule protects students and teachers alike from these powerful human emotions that can wreak such havoc. At the same time, it's important to encourage all instructors to talk freely about any possible emotional attachments taking place. We are all human, and such feelings deserve attention; they should not get swept under the rug.

I am speaking from experience. Long ago I struck up a relationship with a student before the agreed-upon six-month time frame was up. This woman was a therapist who understood the dynamics of transference quite well, as did I. After we spoke to some of the original founders of this training, they agreed with reservations that we were being adult and responsible by communicating to them and to each other what was happening in our hearts and minds before acting. Despite their warnings, we decided to go forward with the relationship.

After a short period of wonderland romance, the bottom fell out, as the projections could no longer hold up to reality. Bitterness quickly ensued as we saw each other as the humans we really were, not as the projected heroes and what-not that we had fantasized each other to be. To our credit, despite this rocky start, the relationship endured for 13 years and even included marriage. We are no longer together but remain good friends, and both agree that whether we were right for each other or not, our relationship was built on very shaky ground from the start due to how we came together.

Transference, when dealt with consciously and appropriately, is a productive teaching tool that can facilitate dramatic breakthroughs in students and change their lives forever. However, it requires a great deal of emotional awareness and maturity to use it as such.

Clearly, the FAST Defense instructor team really has its work cut out for it. A multitude of challenges present themselves in leading students through this unique and powerful learning process. It takes a good deal of time and effort to cultivate a fine-tuned team of coaches and bulletmen, but the rewards merit the effort. A first-class team of instructors will produce consistent results time and time again and literally change the lives of the students who walk through the doors of their classrooms.

Chapter 10

The Healing Power of FAST Defense

Much has been learned over the years of the widespread phenomenon called post-traumatic stress disorder (PTSD). War veterans have served as a rich test environment for uncovering the psychological difficulties of adapting to normal life following exposure to the many horrors of the battlefield. Many veteran soldiers and marines require intensive therapy to effectively return to a life where killing and constant hypervigilance from fear of being killed are not a part of daily life. Unfortunately, a fair number of these people are never able to make the shift and live out the remainder of their lives in a tortured existence, with sleeplessness, nightmares, flashbacks, and more as constant companions.

PTSD is not partial to veterans of military battles. It often afflicts people who have been abused physically and/or emotionally and can significantly impair their ability to deal with stressful situations that rekindle old traumas. Unfortunately, the most commonly prescribed treatment, talk therapy, is usually not enough to reverse PTSD, although it is an important aspect of recovery. The good news is that modern science has identified the brain action that is disrupted through PTSD, and with proper adrenal stress response training we can (and have) helped many people to literally reprogram their brains to work correctly again, enabling them to deal with stressful situations that would have sent them into a catatonic state in the past.

Let's take a rudimentary glimpse into how PTSD works. First, it's important to understand that PTSD can result from any number of situations where a person experiences intense fear and some level of powerlessness. Children are highly susceptible to PTSD when forced to endure a frightening situation where they may have no or little power or control. Parental abuse, whether physical or verbal, can dramatically affect a child's ability to deal with stress for the rest of their lives. But the fear and powerlessness don't necessarily have to occur repeatedly for PTSD to occur. When a dog bites a child, for instance, the victim is often hardwired to a lifetime fear of canines. Teenagers and adults can likewise suffer from PTSD as the result of a single victimization in which they are made to feel powerless. Why is this so?

BRAIN HIGH ROAD/LOW ROAD

Of the two parts of the brain, the low road is the most relevant to understanding PTSD because it is where this harmful behavioral conditioning is stored. PTSD reactions to stress are not conscious brain functions. A person does not *choose* to freeze like a deer in the headlights or respond to a threat with any of the other negative behaviors that typically occur in a PTSD flashback. The response occurs no matter how much the person would like to think or wish it away. Think of it as a hardwiring of the lower brain that presents itself anytime a stressful situation occurs that in any way resembles the original trauma that created it. Interestingly enough, the original trauma doesn't have to be an assault by another human. Virtually any scary situation can hardwire PTSD into the unwary victim if the event does not go well.

Many years ago in the military, I did some rather intense training in the jungles of Asia. While on these ventures my team and I came across some nasty creatures, the likes of which most people have nightmares about. One evening we were just outside a primitive jungle village that looked like it was right out of *National Geographic*. Our orders were to recon the area and not disturb the local people in any way. We did our job and dug in for the night inside a small circle of trees that provided adequate cover. After eating our typical C-rat (combat rations) dinner and posting the guard schedule, we hunkered down for the night. Around 1 a.m., the guard on fire watch woke me up to tell me that something in the trees above us was really spooking him. As I awoke and my eyes adjusted, I saw in the moonlight what looked like a parade of giant ants streaming across the tangled web of tree limbs that served as a sort of roof for our cover.

It took a moment to discern what this midnight aberration really was, and when I did, it sent a chill racing up my spine. Rats! Hundreds, if not thousands, of jungle rats were stirring and coming alive in the trees above us. The sight of them literally froze us all in place, although a few colorful expletives did manage to escape our mouths. My paralysis was suddenly broken when a few of them dropped to the ground. To this day I vividly remember one of these airborne rats landing on my right leg and scampering up the entire length of my body and off my left shoulder as I involuntarily jerked my head out of the way, unleashing an unearthly scream. (Rationally I don't believe this was a bloodthirsty rat going for my throat, but in the moment it might as well have been, as far as my low-road brain was concerned.) In a flash, my deadly elite marine recon team was up and screaming like young girls, scrambling to get the heck out of that small copse of trees to relative safety. Fortunately, none of us were bitten because the rats were much more interested in the C-rat cans we had foolishly left out in the open. But in the adrenal fear rush, we quickly forgot all about our orders for "silent vigilance." The primitive survival flight reaction simply took over.

This event caused no end of laughter as we later retold the story, and in each retelling the rats grew in number and stature. But the end result for most of us was an ingrained, irrational terror of the furry little creatures. The fact that jungle rats can be rabid added to the phobia, but we would have been terrified regardless. There is no doubt that we got a good dose of PTSD from the experience. How do I know? Because months later in a similar jungle, we had another such encounter that evoked the same type of reaction, but this time it was intensified due to the PTSD induced by the first experience. (Yes, it only gets better, folks!)

In this situation we had decided to set up for the evening on an uncovered hilltop bordering the jungle. There was no way we were going to get rained on by rats this time. (Note how past traumatic events can affect even much of our cognitive thinking.) Foolishly, we left our finished C-rat cans out again, thinking that we were safe. Once again the guard sounded an early-morning alarm, and this time we all woke up with a start! Upon awakening I reflexively jerked my head skyward like a trained seal to see where the threat was, just as I had the time before. This time, however, it came from a different direction. The hilltop we were sleeping on was a huge mound of old elephant grass that had piled up over centuries. The rats evidently occupied a web of pathways underneath the mound. Before we knew it, the ground literally came alive with rats pouring out of their unseen holes to get at our food cans. If the previous scenario had been scary, then suffice it to say that this was a horror show of epic proportion. Of course, the rats again merely wanted the food and had no interest in us. But because of PTSD, we reacted with even greater terror and ran for our lives.

Afterward we were all shaken to the core, though we had widely differing accounts of the event as a result of the adrenaline rush. (Adrenaline's effects on different people's ability to observe incidents under stress varies widely. Police encounter this all the time as they attempt to make sense of radically different accounts of the same traumatic event from different eyewitnesses.) It took many hours to calm down, and we got no more sleep that night. Nor did we joke about the incident the way we did the first time. To this day, I still hate rats. In fact, even mice can give my heart a good jump when they scurry past me.

Centipedes affect me the same way, thanks to an incident that took place during a military training exercise in Hawaii. Sleeping under cover along a road where the enemy military units were supposed to travel the next day, I didn't realize that a huge centipede had crawled inside my pants for warmth during the cool night. When the guard woke us up in the early morning, my movement caused the slumbering critter to viciously bite the inside of my thigh. My teammates watched in stunned silence as I frantically rolled around, slamming my fist into my groin area with no idea what was causing the sudden, sharp pain like a barbed spike being driven into my flesh by a hammer. Finally, the monstrous little bugger slithered out of my pant leg and into the brush, imprinting a multilegged image of extreme revulsion upon my mind forever. I did manage to stay quiet that time so as not to compromise our position, but you'd better believe that the mere sight of a centipede still provokes quite a reaction from me even today, 25 years later! (Not to mention it took me years to live that one down among my well-entertained buddies.)

The point is, the negative conditioning of PTSD can occur much more easily than we might believe, and it profoundly impacts our ability to deal with future stressful situations. Virtually any intense situation that does not have a good outcome can cause PTSD, and even events that turn out okay but initially invoke a feeling of very intense fear can cause it. Although I survived the gang attack on my marine base that I spoke of earlier, the terror I felt as it was happening carried over into recurrent nightmares of being chased by gangs of attackers. The residual fear also led me to curtail social activities where the possibility of a gang attack might exist (which could be considered good common sense, though my actions were motivated more by fear than reason).

PTSD is a low road brain phenomenon. As mentioned previously, the low road is comprised of the lymbic system, which is our emotional center, and the amygdala, where past emotional responses both negative and positive, are stored. Thus, the low road brain is predominant during intensely stressful and scary situations. It is also the most difficult part of the brain to train, because in order to condition the low road brain to respond in a different way, fear and stress must be elicited and properly worked through to a successful outcome. If the training is not conducted properly, an even deeper pattern of PTSD can be hardwired into the brain, causing more harm than help. But if the training is done correctly, past trauma can be literally cleared out and replaced with new, empowering responses to fear that can remain for a lifetime.

In fact, scenario-based adrenal stress response training enabled me to work through the PTSD that resulted from the gang attacks I have experienced. Not only do I no longer consciously fear gang attacks (though I do have a healthy respect for their danger), even my dreams have changed radically. Now, whenever I am accosted by groups of attackers in my dreams, I can seriously kick butt. This illustrates the depth of this technology's ability to affect the subconscious mind. Virtually thousands of students have worked through PTSD in the courses we teach using this amazingly simple yet incredibly powerful process.

ACQUAINTANCE ATTACKS

FBI statistics reveal that more than 80 percent of attacks on women are committed by someone they know. This is good news and bad news. The good news is that, despite what we see in movies like *Psycho* and *Silence of the Lambs*, most predators who attack women are not the bloodthirsty demons of our worst nightmares. The bad news is that since they tend to be acquaintances or even people their victims might care about, the boundaries are much more vague and the patterns of socio-conditioning all the more difficult to fight against. It is one thing when the assailant is a stranger who suddenly materializes in a dark alley and the attack is obviously on, and quite another when it's a coworker, friend, boyfriend, or spouse with whom things are beginning to go very awry. Women succumb to this common threat all too often, and unless they give themselves permission to break through denial, accept the reality of their plight, and take appropriate defensive action, no amount of tactical self-defense training will change that pattern of behavior. This is much easier said than done.

Date rape is rampant among young women and is one of the most difficult situations to prepare them to deal with. A woman must break through a huge amount of socio-conditioning to effectively stop a person she cares about from hurting her. The need for love is a major driving human need that, sadly, can allow people to accept abuse that leaves a lot of damage in its wake. Simply threatening to withhold love is a form of abuse that effectively manipulates and controls people in harmful ways that can drastically alter the course of their lives. Add to this the effects of alcohol and/or drugs (which are prevalent in the vast majority of these cases), and the problems are compounded on both sides. Under the influence of drugs or alcohol, young guys often end up doing things they would not have done sober, and young women find themselves less capable of determining when a situation is turning for the worse and taking a stand when and if they do. If date rape drugs are a factor, they may not be capable of doing either.

Case in point: Susan signed up for our course after she was raped by a guy who had been her boyfriend for two years prior to the assault. He was normally a nice guy but would get mean after a few drinks, she told us. (We hear this way too often!) They had been out to dinner, and he wanted her to spend the evening with him instead of going home to her apartment. Her intuitive voices were firing off "don't do it" signals. But he had just spent a load of money on the dinner and was being very persuasive. The final straw was when he stated that she must not love him as much as he loved her and threatened to pull out of the relationship if this was how she was going to treat him. She finally agreed to go to his house for a short while but stipulated that he needed to take her home later that night. It took him about an hour and another two drinks before he made his Jekyll-and-Hyde switch, telling her to get into his bed. Susan had also been drinking and feebly tried to resist, which made him so angry he threatened her with bodily harm. Shocked by this unusually sudden and vicious change of personality, she froze in terror and confusion as he raped her. As is so typical in these cases, it took Susan months to finally admit that she was a victim and accept that the rape was not her fault. Her belief was that she had led him on and indirectly asked to be raped because she didn't do enough to stop it. Worse than the actual rape was the shame she felt for allowing it to occur. The only means of survival she knew was to shut the doors on the horrible guilt and shame, hiding it away in the veiled secrecy that so many women use as a survival mechanism in this often-callous, male-dominated world. The first people she had ever spoken to about it were the staff and students of her class.

Through our training Susan came to realize that the fault was not hers and that she didn't deserve this at all. Like so many victims, she felt responsible for her attack because she had failed to stop her perpetrator. After training in FAST Defense, she realized that she did the best she could with what she had available at the time. By gaining an understanding of the myriad conditioned factors that led her to become a victim, she, like so many of our students, was finally able to let go of the guilt and shame that had bound her to the event since it occurred. She changed dramatically, both physically and emotionally. The course gave her the tools to take back her life. You would not have recognized the woman who came in the door at the beginning of class as the one who left. Today she volunteers her time at a local rape crisis center and specializes in educating young women and teens on the dynamics of date rape and how to keep it from happening. Having transformed her fear and pain into power, she is now making a difference in the lives of many other young women.

Of course, the other side of the coin is the conditioning that young men are getting in this society. A lot of resources are going into helping women who have been raped, but very few address why these guys are committing these acts in the first place. Although I believe most guys are decent human beings, there is a lot of detrimental socio-conditioning taking place through prevalent influences like video games, movies, and TV with much more violent and sexual content than anything that our parents and grandparents were exposed to. Very little parental or societal energy is being directed toward teaching young boys what sexual behavior is appropriate and what is not, so they are figuring it out as they go along, and often not very well. Until these issues are addressed on a large scale, society is merely applying an elaborate Band-Aid to the problem in focusing on post-rape solutions. Programs such as FAST Defense create a rare opportunity for young men to hear firsthand from their female classmates how sexual assault negatively impacts them, sometimes drastically. These courses are highly effective proactive solutions to this problem because they serve to repudiate the erroneous ideas that are so ingrained in young men by society and by their peers.

BATTERED WOMAN SYNDROME

Most people cannot understand why any woman would stay in an abusive relationship year after year, allowing herself to be denigrated emotionally and often abused physically. I was incredulous myself when I first heard how common this situation is. It was only after repeatedly hearing similar stories of this same cycle of abuse that the fog started to lift and I came to accept that battered woman syndrome is a very real problem and one of the toughest cycles to break in our society.

The interpersonal dynamics that engender such a relationship are subtle and very tricky to catch for the unwary victim. Typically, the abuser starts off by presenting himself as a nice guy who is charismatic and seemingly quite sensitive. But this veneer wears off in time to reveal a man who is very insecure and fearful, needing to control the very people he claims to love. After gaining a woman's trust, he will often gently coerce her into giving in to him on some matter, thereby compromising herself in some way. This is not the same as the healthy compromise that occurs in any normal relationship. It is a compromise of the heart, where her gut tells her it is not right, but she does it anyway because he makes her feel she would be less of a person if she didn't concede. "If you really loved me . . ." is how such coercion often goes. Any woman with low self-esteem to begin with is particularly susceptible to this ploy. Such a woman is typically raised in an abusive environment or in an emotional void, and this pattern may be all she knows. Again, the need for love is a primal urge in humans, and many people will do anything to get it, even when that "love" is the cause of physical abuse (and even death) in many cases.

Once the initial compromise is made, the door is open to future concessions. Each time the perpetrator will draw his victim in and get her to give up something of greater value or compromise her values even further. As the relationship progresses, he breaks down her spirit by constantly berating her, using any point of vulnerability he can find. She is allowed to make fewer and fewer choices as he becomes more and more controlling. Under such a barrage of negativity, many women fume inside if they have enough self-respect left to do so. But after each horrible, belittling incident, her perpetrator returns with smiles or even tears of regret, promising never to do it again. So the honeymoon phase is rekindled and the flowers arrive—for a while, anyway. And then the cycle repeats, each time growing in intensity. Finally, numbness sets in as a survival mechanism that enables the woman to endure the endless cycle of abuse, reconciliation, and more abuse. Among the debilitating effects is intense shame for allowing such abuse to occur and a feeling of being helpless to change it. Such shame ensures her silence—and the continued success of her abuser. (I would be remiss not to note here that men are battered by their wives in this same way in far more cases than most people realize. These men are victims of the same denigration and shame that keep women silent in so many cases.)

Sadly, it's not uncommon for women to stay in this cycle forever. Women also tend to take responsibility for the feelings of their abusers, hoping beyond reasonable hope that they can somehow change their spouse's behavior or believing that the abuse was their own fault in the first place. Although women often won't fight for themselves, they will typically do anything to protect their children, and thus some finally break out of the abuse when their children become directly involved. (Of course, any children involved are always victims in these situations, either directly or indirectly.)

In my line of work I have come to realize that arming a woman who is in a battering relationship to defend herself physically is a real razor's edge. Unless she is totally committed and prepared to fight back against her abuser, we may just be sending her into a fire armed with a bucket of jet fuel. Factor in the high percentage of abusers who disregard court-issued restraining orders and return to abuse their victims further, and you start to get the picture. Even if these women do successfully defend themselves in an abusive incident, they still have to deal with hubby or boyfriend days or weeks later unless he has been incarcerated, and at that point he may be more of a threat than ever.

Help for such a woman must come from a variety of resources. First, it is essential that she remove herself (and any children in the picture) from the abusive environment if at all possible. Secondly, individual and group therapy with a specialist in PTSD is crucial. By "specialist" I am not referring to the slew of well-meaning but sadly uninformed ministers and counselors who will advise her to follow the traditional route of "stand by your man." Emotional guidance must come from someone who fully comprehends the volatile and extremely complicated issues at play in domestic violence. Just as important to the woman seeking to break out of the cycle of abuse is that she receives total validation for the wide range of emotions—from fear to sadness and grief to anger—that she will inevitably experience. Anyone who is judgmental or punitive should be removed from the picture entirely. These victims have often already endured years of emotional torment as a result of being told they are bad and wrong, and they do not need any more of that nonsense. They should be held with loving hands and allowed to feel as safe as humanly possible at this crucial point in the healing process.

All this takes time, of course; the relationship dynamics that both sides have been playing out cannot be reversed overnight. Furthermore, once the healing has begun for the woman, going back into the trenches is frightening and dangerous. Quite often, her returning to a previously abusive relationship with a brittle newfound sense of confidence gained from such therapy will cause her perpetrator to escalate his abusive behavior very rapidly once he senses that his well-contrived theater of operation has been threatened.

In my experience, scenario-based adrenal stress response training is the perfect final step in the healing process. I have worked with a multitude of battered women survivors over the years, and I know that by the time most of them finally walk through the doors of a self-defense course they have won half the battle already by overcoming the intense degree of socio-conditioning that allowed them to simply put up with the abuse. Although still mired in fear, they have reached a point where their anger has overcome their victim mentality. This marks the beginning of their transformation from "victim" to "survivor," and it is a very healthy and powerful time for them because it is literally the dawn of a new chapter in their lives.

FAST Defense has proven to be a very powerful way to facilitate such transformation. A skilled instructor team can lead a student through a process that re-creates a past situation in which she was a victim. Once the student is adequately prepared, she relives the abuse as choreographed by the staff, and this time she comes out the victor. Psychologists who have taken part in this process have stated that this customized scenario alone is worth years of talk therapy. In my experience, the transformations that occur are highly charged emotionally and nothing short of life changing. Sharing in the power and beauty of a prior victim taking back her life is the most rewarding experience I have ever had. Such a moving display of human spirit impacts the entire class and staff as well as the student herself. Even more importantly, many students have left abusive situations entirely and experienced extraordinary healing after such a metamorphosis.

The Story of Mary

A number of years back, Mary came to our course on the advice of the local women's shelter. I will never forget her sunken eyes and stooped posture as she walked in the door. During check-in, she couldn't make eye contact with anyone, and her voice squeaked like that of a toddler every time she spoke. She was there to gain the confidence to finally leave the man who had battered her emotionally and physically for more than 12 years. Her daughter was now a teenager, and the abuser had begun to turn his amorous intentions her way, which finally horrified Mary enough to take action.

At one point Mary confided to the group how she originally came to be in this abusive situation. Her husband was a recovering alcoholic when they met. With a few years of sobriety under his belt, he had found a good job and seemed quite ready for a stable relationship. Having grown up in an alcoholic and verbally abusive environment, Mary was happy to have found someone who showed a genuine caring for her. They were married, and soon she was pregnant with their child.

Following the birth of their daughter, Mary's husband began to act agitated and distant. After much cajoling, she got him to admit that he felt alone and feared that she cared more about the baby than she did him. Despite her assurances to the contrary, he grew even more distant and started coming home later and later. Greatly concerned, Mary tried in vain to get him to stop his late-night carousing. Finally, he said that if she wanted him to stop, she would have to agree to take a trip with him and leave the baby behind. Disregarding her gut feeling that she should not leave her newborn in the hands of others, she acquiesced. Away they went on a vacation to Mexico, placing their two-month-old daughter in the less-than-capable hands of Mary's sister-in-law.

In Mexico things went from bad to worse. On day one hubby was very loving and affectionate and drew her into somewhat forgetting that she had a very bad feeling about all of this. But by the second evening he began drinking, and the verbal abuse again reared its ugly head. Suddenly, this semicrazed man she had never known before started hurling at her all the things she had ever done wrong in his eyes, verbally attacking her for loving the baby more than she had ever loved him, and berating her for being a horrible mother to leave her newborn at home with someone who was not completely trustworthy. Dazed and confused, Mary again pleaded with him to stop, reminding him that it was his idea to leave their daughter with his sister. He left the hotel in a tirade and didn't come home that night.

When he showed up the next morning, disheveled and still intoxicated, he cried at her feet, apologizing profusely and promising never to be abusive again. That evening he behaved himself. But the next day he was right back to being abusive, this time with even more ferocity. He claimed that if she loved him she would go out with him to a bar, where they would find another woman to have sex with. Horror-struck, she refused, and off again he went. Despite feeling sick and nauseous, she felt guilty for letting him down more than anything. The next evening she agreed to go out with him, even though she was sickened to the core. Fortunately, he ended up getting so intoxicated that he was cut off, and they went back to the hotel for the final evening of their "vacation."

All the way home he apologized and said he would seek treatment for his drinking and anger issues. After a short stint in Alcoholics Anonymous, he seemed to be back on track. Then gradually the cycle began again. And so it continued, up and down for 12 years. Each time he got abusive he was profusely sorry afterward and promised he would never do it again. And always he broke his promise. The debasing criticism would begin, followed by the drinking and the late nights. Each time Mary gave in to his demands to appease him, he would push her a step further. In tears, she bravely confided that she had allowed him to talk her into doing things that she could never tell anyone about. Her shame kept her silent. She had always hung on to the hope that this time it would be different. But it never changed, and in fact it grew worse. She had learned to numb out and accept her plight, because deep down she felt it was her fault anyway.

It all changed for her when their daughter came of age. One evening, in a drunken stupor, her husband demanded that they all get into bed. Suddenly, the years of being trampled upon emotionally and physically were transformed into pissed-off mama bear fury, and she hit him so hard with a chair that he was knocked unconscious. Hurriedly, she grabbed her daughter and a few possessions and ran out the door to a friend's house. Her friend helped her call the local shelter. The next morning she was finally on her way to the recovery she needed so badly. Eventually she ended up in our course on the recommendation of her therapist, who had assessed that it was time for Mary's next level of healing.

In this weekend-intensive course for survivors of abuse, we all witnessed in Mary the rebirth of a woman taking back her life after enduring incredible adversity. Her body language began to change; her head and eyes burned with a new intensity and fire. On Sunday she walked out on the mat to re-create a particularly shaming incident. Crying intensely but reacting with purpose and laser-beam focus, she fought for herself and for her daughter, and that day she took back her life. Mary left us that evening proud and strong, a woman who had finally realized that she was not only a good and loving mother but also a beautiful woman in her power. Weeks later we received a letter from her saying that she was living life on her own terms and would never be a victim again.

Mary's experience illustrates how scenario-based adrenal stress response training goes well beyond imparting self-defense skills. In fact, one could say that it falls more into the realm of self-improvement and life skills than anything else. Any way you look at it, this technology has the means to dramatically change the lives of people who have experienced all manner of victimization. It has the power to reverse the debilitating effects of PTSD and change their lives forever.

Chapter 11

Specialized Adrenal Stress Response Training Applications

Although the concepts and techniques of FAST Defense are geared toward the general self-defense market, there are a number of specific applications for this type of training that include and extend far beyond self-defense. Remember, adrenal stress response training is about much more than facing the padded attacker and executing full-force strikes to his head and groin. The real power of this training lies in helping people to respond effectively in any sort of adrenal stress-inducing situation. Following are examples of some specific groups for whom adrenal stress response training has proven particularly beneficial, as well as some particularly violent scenarios that are addressed by advanced adrenal response training courses.

LAW ENFORCEMENT AND MILITARY PERSONNEL

There is perhaps no group that could benefit from

adrenal stress response training more than law enforcement officers, who put their lives on the line for the rest of us every day. Yet many officers' training is sadly lacking in this regard, aside from a brief introduction many of them receive in their initial academy training. Even this is typically performed by well-meaning but ill-trained instructors using inferior training methods and equipment. Granted, special units such as SWAT often get much better training, and there are some very qualified training regimens that these and other elite units are privy to. But the average law enforcement officer on patrol usually gets the short end of the stick when it comes to training that will truly prepare him or her for the rigors of police duty.

Typically, it consists mostly of on-the-job training where officers are thrust into hostile situations and simply learn over time how to deal with the adrenaline and fear that anyone would feel in the intense situations they often face. Watch any of the current *COPS* shows to get an idea of what these real-life heroes face on a daily basis. Of course, on TV it can look easy and under control, and perhaps it is. But you don't see rookie cops sent out to the hard cases on these shows. These guys and gals have been around the block a few times. Veteran officers are experts at dealing with the adrenal rush because they have learned how to respond appropriately over time through trial and error. It's interesting to note that seasoned police officers rarely get into physical confrontations because they have instinctively learned to practice the awareness and verbal defense strategies outlined in this book. They have learned well that through assertive demeanor and skillful interaction, most situations can be de-escalated and stopped before they ever become violent. It works for civilians when done correctly, and it sure works for law enforcement officers. But the new officers on the beat don't have the benefit of this experience, and because lack of seniority often denies them the better shifts and locations, it's frequently the rookies who end up dealing with the worst-case scenarios. It is these new officers who need adrenal stress response training more than anyone.

One of the problems we have with getting adrenal stress response training to the law enforcement community has been the misconception that it is strictly about striking full force to vulnerable areas on the attacker. For liability reasons, officers are restricted—sometimes to a ridiculous degree—in what they can do physically to the bad guys out on the street. In some police forces it's a sad fact that officers are not allowed to react physically at all until their lives are seriously threatened. Even then, many are not allowed to protect themselves for fear of legal retribution from the very lawbreakers they are working to protect us from. Sadly, this is sometimes the result of previous inappropriate, overly aggressive responses by rookie cops who hadn't yet acquired the street skill to stay calm in very stressful situations. Just as sad is the flip side of the coin, where a relatively new officer underreacts and is hurt or even killed in the line of duty during an intense confrontation with the bad guys.

The beauty of FAST Defense is that it trains people how to work within the intense adrenal rush, stay cognizant, and respond appropriately and responsibly to the given situation, similar to what veteran cops of many years of walking a beat achieve. Just as the veteran cops typically don't need to use physical force, neither do most graduates of a single half-day FAST Defense seminar. So even though we train our civilians to hit full force to vital targets that are not acceptable for law enforcement officers to use unless their lives are truly in danger, the experience of flipping that switch and going full force when necessary provides the adrenal stress conditioning to keep them from having to use that level of force more often than not. And when they do need to use force, it is with more awareness of the appropriate level of intensity and with greater skill and care.

Routine scenario-based adrenal stress response training for officers would prevent a great deal of police brutality cases because officers so trained would be much less likely to respond in an overly aggressive, knee-jerk manner. The infamous Rodney King incident and so many others might well never have occurred had the officers received adequate training to deal with the intense adrenaline rush they experienced in these situations.

FAST Defense offers various new courses designed to work within the legal parameters of the acceptable defensive techniques prescribed for police officers. These courses are gaining acceptance in the law enforcement community, and the officers who have experienced them rave about the experience. Most express sadness that this training was not more available when they were rookies and needed it most. It is now, and we are working hard to bring these training concepts to the good men and women charged with keeping us safe.

I am absolutely convinced that just as adrenal stress response training is invaluable for police officers, it could dramatically increase the proficiency of combat soldiers and save many lives. It would also be very effective to help returning military personnel recover from the post-traumatic stress that so many suffer from. Unfortunately, budgets are stretched thin in wartime, and it's a challenge for the military to provide enough bullets and Band-Aids, much less auxiliary hand-to-hand combat training.

ATHLETES

A good number of FAST Defense graduates have expressed to me how FAST Defense has improved their powers to crank it up during a particular athletic event. One college hockey player who took the course, for instance, noted that he is now less compelled to fight during games because his adrenaline is more under his control. He has found that he can focus his adrenaline with laser-beam precision to perform at levels he had never achieved before.

I have observed this same thing with my son, Jeremy, on the lacrosse field. He has taken FAST Defense classes since he was 8 years old, and I see this experience applied directly to his actions on the field. He can focus his spirit and will far better than most kids his age or even years older. At 16 he is a star player and team leader with a promising future. If coaches spent a fraction of the time on spirit training as they do on technique training, I believe athletes would very quickly experience exponential gains in their ability to perform under the stress and nervousness that are inherent to any athletic contest. If self-defense comes down to 10 percent technique and 90 percent spirit, it follows that the same applies in sports.

CHILDREN

Think back to when you were a youngster. On summer vacation you probably headed out to play with your friends immediately after breakfast and often didn't return home until dinnertime. There was almost no end to the freedom. Now think of letting your child do that in today's world. Most of us wouldn't even consider allowing our children such freedom, even in most rural communities. The world has changed, and unfortunately it would not be prudent to allow today's children the liberties that we had just a few decades ago. The press bombards us daily with alerts to the sexual predators in our midst, as well as rampant drug use and the increasing prevalence of weapons on our streets and violence in our schools. Although the risk may be blown out of proportion in many areas, there can be no denying that in general, the children of today face greater risks than ever before.

Many self-defense courses for children are essentially lectures. Perhaps a police officer or fireman is invited to their classroom to speak. Although lecture can be somewhat effective when teaching children, it only affects the brain, overlooking the physical and emotional aspects of learning. Thus, most lecture-style instruction does not stick for the average child, nor does it prepare him or her to react to a real-life threat.

In the early '90s, I began designing a program for children ages 6 to 12 at the urging of several adult FAST Defense graduates. Many of them were teachers and other professionals who had firsthand experience with the myriad stressful situations kids face. With their guidance and a great deal of research, I developed a series of seminars for kids. EZ Defense for Children (provided by the National Association of Professional Martial Artists) and FAST C.A.T.S. (Child Assertiveness Training Series) provide playful, age-appropriate versions of the same scenario-based experiential teaching methods we use to train adults in FAST Defense. With often-miraculous effects, this training has equipped thousands of children to cope with a range of threats, from dealing with bullies to thwarting potential abductions. The skills taught in these programs range from awareness to verbal defense to physical defense as a last resort.

The very first FAST C.A.T.S. class I taught in 1996 produced a successful abduction defense by the daughter of a good friend of mine. My friend is forever grateful, and his daughter has grown into a strong, confident young lady. We all hope and pray that our children won't ever need these skills. But if they do, such training is beyond priceless!

And the benefits go far beyond self-defense: each time a child successfully takes assertive action, his or her self-esteem grows exponentially. Now a high school student with eight years of adrenal stress response training under his belt, my son's confidence levels are amazing. He is of no interest to bullies and even helps his friends prevent the myriad forms of harassment perpetrated by the bullies in his school. His behavior enables me to trust him to be safe and responsible, which allows him the freedom to do activities many kids are not allowed to do. This further increases his esteem and my parental trust. (How different this is from my own experience growing up, where the opposite was usually the case!)

MARTIAL ARTISTS

Although the martial arts world is more open to change than ever, there is still a good bit of denial regarding the need for adrenal stress response training. Many martial artists look at adrenal stress response training as ridiculous crap that has no place in martial arts or self-defense. The typical argument is that they already know self-defense from their martial arts training and don't need to learn whatever this stuff is about. Others make fun of the padded armor, and many balk at the verbal abuse that the male instructors use at various times in the courses. Nonetheless, from the advent of this unique training methodology, there has been one very powerful validation: virtually everyone who has ever tried adrenal stress response training like FAST Defense and RMCAT has raved about it. There remains considerable criticism about this methodology, but none of it comes from anyone who has actually ever experienced it. I have never had a single student come through a course give it anything less than a glowing review afterward. In my 17 years of teaching thousands of students, I have yet to get even a neutral response from someone. Moreover, the martial art instructors who have tried this type of training invariably report that the experience has changed for the better how they teach. FAST Defense is not a replacement for the martial arts. It is the missing link in providing students with important skills outside of the traditional martial arts teaching paradigm, and it builds a bridge for them to actually apply what they learn in the traditional environment to real-life altercations. Many progressive martial art schools now incorporate adrenal stress response training into their curriculum and testing so that by the time a student is a black belt he or she will have had adrenal stress response experience that could only have been gained the hard way otherwise.

Think for a moment why most people join the martial arts in the first place. Although a rare few do so for the sheer joy of the martial arts, most are motivated by a desire to gain confidence and greater control over their lives. As a young martial artist, I was intrigued with the image of the wise old master who was fearless in the face of the most frightening adversity. Fear was such a factor in my own life that I bought into the notion that the martial arts would make me fearless, giving me control over my emotions as well as my body. Although I did gain some confidence from moving through the ranks to black belt and beyond, fear still held its grip on me every time I got into intense confrontations. I never succeeded in attaining that "wise old master" state through either the martial arts or the military training I received. Although I did reach a high level of physical prowess, underlying it was always an unease that one day I might get tested by the wrong person and my fragile sense of personal security would come crashing down.

Through the FAST Defense methodology, my internal struggle began to undergo a dramatic change. An inner strength developed that was totally different from the old cocky bravado that I had used as protection for so many years. I became calmer and found that I no longer worried about getting into confrontations. In fact, I really don't think about them at all anymore. Oddly enough, it is extremely rare that I find myself in any sort of challenge or confrontation these days. I believe this is because I project good, assertive communication to everyone I meet, and because I treat them with respect, they in turn respect me. On the infrequent occasion when a confrontation does arise, I'm able to deal with it quickly and appropriately before the situation has a chance to become volatile.

When you come to believe at a heart level that not only can you take care of yourself but you are also worth taking care of, your self-respect goes out like sonar to the jerks and predators of the world. They sense your quiet assuredness, and it usually prompts them to leave you alone or to treat you with respect because you command it. Life will always be challenging, and fear will always be a part of those challenges. But when you accept the fear and learn to work with it, it loses its power over you. This, I believe, is what I was searching for in the lofty image of the wise old master. When you are no longer controlled by fear, you conserve all the immense quantities of energy that you formerly expended to fight against the fear, and you begin to relax.

FAST Defense provides students with the skills to protect and defend themselves, and it enables them to practice those skills under duress in a controlled and safe environment where success is almost a guaranteed result every time. This process, more than any other aspect of their training, gives them the quiet, assured confidence that many of them are seeking in choosing to study the martial arts. For this reason alone, scenario-based adrenal stress response training is perhaps the greatest martial arts training tool that has ever come along, and each year we learn more and get better at combining the richness of traditional martial arts training with this powerful new technology.

Ground Fighting

The mid-1990s marked the debut of the Ultimate Fighting Challenge, produced by the Gracie family of Brazil, who specialized in a unique style of jiu-jitsu. In these no-holds-barred tournaments, stand-up punch-kick fighters were routinely taken to the ground and defeated by the seemingly unstoppable Gracies. This led to a new rage, and ground-fighting schools popped up across the United States as traditional fighters desperately sought to even up the score.

Now, years later, the rage has somewhat subsided, but the Gracies have forever left their mark on the martial arts world. Ground fighting was an important facet of defense that was not adequately addressed in many traditional Asian fighting arts. But do these same principles apply in street fights?

The common wisdom is that most fights end up on the ground, yet in my personal experience in literally dozens of fights, only once did I ever end up on the ground. It was a classically ridiculous situation where a drunk called me out of a bar to fight. Leading an entourage of characters like something out of the movie *Roadhouse*, the two of us "took it outside" to the back of the bar. I was a young buck of 19 at the time and was pretty nervous as the macabre scene unfolded.

This other guy was obnoxiously drunk and had pissed off a number of bar patrons, so as the token local martial artist, I was the emotional favorite of the unruly onlookers. It did feel good to have the mob on my side, misguided though it was. We stood there a while as my opponent spewed out drunken obscenities but made no opening move. I was getting fed up with the whole thing and really just wanted to end it so I could go back in and have another beer. Finally, he took a long, slow-motion roundhouse swing at me. In fairly good shape and a trained karateka, I moved in and straight-punched him in the jaw. It all seemed like a slow-motion movie as my fist skipped off his chin, barely nicking him. To my disbelief, he collapsed to the ground and landed flat on his back. Stunned and not knowing what else to do, I dropped onto his chest and started halfheartedly smacking his face. The whole thing seemed surreal, and after a short while, my friends thankfully pulled me off the poor drunken guy.

With a detached awareness, I noticed blood all over my hands and shirt. It wasn't mine. What an amazing and impressive victory for me, right? Well, the truth was that when our drunken lad swung at me, he lost his balance on some ice (it was winter in New England), and my chip shot was enough to throw him off balance even more and put him on the ground. Upon landing, he cut his hand on a piece of glass, accounting for the blood. The "victory" was a fluke caused by nothing I did at all, but by a bizarre set of circumstances. His face wasn't even bruised where I had been hitting him.

In my experience, most fights go to the ground because the participants don't really know how to fight, as was the case here. Succumbing to the adrenal rush, people tend to flail ineffectually. Eventually, a clinch ensues because most fighters exhibit the overly fast tempo and shortened motion of stress-induced adrenaline. These inept grappling matches often end up on the ground due to the force of gravity more than anything else.

In the years that followed, after I *had* learned how to street fight, not a single altercation that I was involved in ever ended up on the ground. A good stand-up fighter should be able to take care of business without going down (that is, if awareness and verbal skills don't prevent the altercation in the first place). Again, it has been my experience and observation that fights typically do *not* go to the ground if one of the combatants has any fighting skill whatsoever. In fact, many self-defense experts would agree that the ground is not a good place to be in a street fight at all. Master Ricardo Murgel, former coach of Brazil's national jiu-jitsu team with a 7th-degree black belt in Brazilian jiu-jitsu and now a world-renowned combat jiu-jitsu instructor and law enforcement trainer, emphatically states that he will avoid going to the ground at all costs in a street situation. (This is quite a statement coming from Murgel; you simply do not want to let this guy get his hands on you—on the ground or anywhere!)

Regardless, there are situations that do end up on the ground. Many female victims in particular have experienced being helpless on the ground. Women in general have not had the same wrestling experience that guys often get while growing up. And if they did, it was probably not a positive experience. So while most of the complicated combat restraints like arm bars and joint locks are very difficult to apply under duress, a basic knowledge of ground-fighting skills is important to have. It's essential to learn how to get someone off you, locate and attack vulnerable areas, and get up and out of there as soon as possible—and to practice doing these things under duress. The argument can also be made that learning ground-fighting skills makes it easier to see such attacks coming and neutralize them.

Although the ground is the last place to be in a street fight, a basic understanding of ground fighting is important.

Sport fighting and no-holds-barred events require the fighter to have ground-fighting skills to be competitive. But there is a big difference between these consensual athletic contests (which still involve *some* rules and safety limits) and real-life altercations (where there are no rules and regulations and where people often get seriously hurt or killed). In FAST Defense we use ground fighting to really amp up the adrenaline intensity level by placing the students in worst-case scenarios that they have to fight their way out of. These very intense scenarios never fail to drive home the concept of 90 percent spirit/10 percent technique. Things get real primitive real fast among trained and untrained ground fighters alike. The reality is that very few of our students will ever have to use those ground-fighting skills. But if they do, they won't be fighting tournament style, tactically looking for strategic arm bars and other restraining holds. They will do whatever they must to get into a dominant position and strike unceasingly to any vulnerable target that presents itself until they can get away safely.

DEFENDING AGAINST ARMED ASSAILANTS

The psychology of dealing with an attacker who has a weapon is quite different than that of dealing with an unarmed one. The mind-set of a typical predator is based on fear, and thus extreme caution is always in order when responding to the threat he presents. The attacker who needs to use a weapon for extra intimidation typically has even greater fear, and thus the danger he poses is all the greater. For the victim, the level of fear is usually greater in an armed attack as well, and for good reason. The one time I was robbed at gunpoint, I was totally paralyzed with fear. Despite the fact that I was with two other tough-guy marines, all I could see were the distinct shapes of the muzzles of really big guns and an indeterminate number of bad guys. I figure it was either five or six, but I was so tunnel-visioned on the guns I can't be sure.

Obviously the risk of severe injury is much greater when a weapon is employed. In FAST Defense we teach that the first line of defense against an armed attacker is to comply if it is a crime of possession. In other words, if he wants something of yours and is willing to use a weapon to get it, the best thing to do is give it up. You can always replace things, but you cannot replace you.

In our weapons defense courses, we rob all of our students so they can experience playing the compliance tactic. When one female graduate of our weapons course was robbed by two armed burglars two blocks from her house just months after she took the course, she very calmly complied as they took her purse and then her jewelry. She actually tried to negotiate when it came time to give up her precious family heirloom wedding ring. Although this is not a generally prescribed tactic, she recounted that she was able to be very clear because of her prior training and felt sure that these men were not intent on harming her. She ended up giving away her ring after they showed that there was no room for negotiating. Afterward, this woman experienced very little of the post-traumatic stress that most people feel in such cases. She attributed this also to her FAST Defense training and her ability to calmly assess the correct action and apply it. In other words, even though she lost her possessions, even precious ones, she did not feel like a victim because she maintained control over herself and responded with conscious awareness and skill.

When to Fight against an Armed Attacker

Although crime statistics indicate that most armed attackers don't have the intent to harm their victims, there are situations where it's clearly a matter of life or death, right there, right then. If someone has plunged a knife into your abdomen, swung a bat at your head, or shot a gun at you, the only viable option you have is to fight for all you are worth. In FAST Defense, we work to instill the survival mind-set in our students that empowers them to take this option when necessary. Victims have survived horrific stabbings, beatings, and even shootings and lived to later prosecute their attackers. If you do have to fight, it's important to be very clear in your mind that you will probably be injured, perhaps quite seriously. The key factor to your survival is your will to keep on going until the bad guy is either gone or out cold. You must be totally committed that no matter what happens to you in the ensuing battle, you will not stop no matter what!

Never Give Up!

If you believe you will survive no matter what happens, you probably will. On the other hand, there were cases of soldiers in Vietnam who had fingers shot off (certainly a frightening but hardly ever a life-threatening wound) and actually died from blood loss because they completely fell apart emotionally. They believed that if they got shot, they would die, and so they did. Conversely, other soldiers received incredibly deadly wounds and survived against all odds because they believed they would.

In 1995 a woman from Boulder, Colorado, survived an attack where she suffered more than 80 stab wounds. Her assault began in the relative safety of town and proceeded to the mountains. Although she was much smaller and physically weaker than her assailant, she never gave up. After fighting off her attacker, she was able to get to a main road and hitch a ride to the hospital. Later that day she was coherent enough to give a good description of the guy to the local police. Two weeks later he was back in jail. He had a long list of prior offenses and was on probation for another armed assault!

In addition to illustrating the importance of the survival mind-set, this harrowing tale also highlights a cardinal rule that we always stress in FAST Defense training: *Never allow yourself to be taken to a secondary location!* If the attacker has the intent to take you to another location, never, ever comply! If you know that an attacker is going to take you somewhere else, at that point your best and only option is to fight like a wild animal or use any means necessary to escape.

According to the 2003 *FBI Uniform Crime Report,* an extremely high percentage of victims (more than 90 percent) are killed after being taken to a secondary location. Think about it: if the place you are initially attacked is not good for him to do what he wants to do to you, that place is exactly where you want to be! You have a better chance of surviving jumping out of a moving car or dodging a bullet than you do at that secondary location. The woman who survived more than 80 stab wounds had allowed herself to be taken to the mountains from the relative safety of town. She was luckier than most.

Tactics for Physical Defense against an Armed Attacker

Again, if an attacker is using a weapon to intimidate you into complying with a robbery, the best thing to do is give up your stuff. But if the assailant is about to use his weapon to harm you or is already attacking you physically, then there is no more room for negotiation: it is time to fight. In FAST Defense the techniques we use to teach our students to physically defend against an armed attacker are very simple because they have to be. Fancy disarms and elaborate techniques are great in the safety of a martial arts class but are not practical in a real fight. Even skilled martial artists don't usually attempt to use their fancy techniques in such a scenario, and if they do, many times their situation becomes worse because the techniques are too complicated to work in the absence of fine motor capability. I specialized in knife, stick, and gun defense in my Filipino martial arts training and became quite good at it. But I have never even considered using these fancy techniques in real situations. The few times I tried it against fellow bulletmen during FAST weapons defense training, I always got the worst of the situation because FAST Defense attackers never fight like sparring partners do in the safe, choreographed environment of the karate classroom; they fight like street predators.

The FAST Defense weapons defense strategies are 1) if possible, run like hell ("run fu" is a great form of self-defense), and 2) if escape is not possible, feign compliance, stay calm and conscious, and wait for the opportunity to strike. The advantage of surprise could literally save your life! If you can get anything in your hand to put between you and the attacker, do so! I had one innovative student run off the mat and pick up a chair during an armed assailant class when I attacked him with a fake knife. He charged at me with that aluminum chair, and it took the fight right out of me! Skilled as I am, I would have been hard-pressed to stick him with my knife even if I had wanted to.

It is highly advisable to get something in your hands should you have to defend against an armed attacker.

When the opportunity to strike comes, the objective is to immobilize the weapon. While the weapon is free, it is a liability! We teach our students to either attack the weapon with another weapon (anything you can get your hands on) or attack with both hands to strike and grab the weapon and weapon hand. Obviously, if it's a knife or gun, you don't want to be grabbing the edge or muzzle. But you also don't want to be grabbing so far up the arm that the attacker can articulate his wrist to still cut or shoot you. That said, it can be better to grab a dangerous part of a weapon and suffer injuries to your hands than to let go and get hurt much worse while trying to renegotiate a better hold in the heat of battle.

In the FAST Defense weapons course, students practice these tactics slowly and safely with each other. The instructors encourage them to try different angles of attack and allow them plenty of practice in controlling the weapon hand and immediately landing a softening knee strike to the attacker's groin. After two hours of this practice, the students then apply the same techniques against the male instructors wearing groin protectors. Once again, the students are attacked at various angles and must swiftly move in to control the weapon and deliver a full-force strike to the instructor's groin. In the final step, the instructor dons his full body armor and attacks the student full force with various weapons and from various angles. The student must respond by cutting off the angle of attack and controlling the weapon and weapon hand *with both hands*. Then he or she must immediately deliver a strike to the attacker's groin to soften him up and avoid an upper-body struggle. Once the padded attacker has taken a few solid groin strikes,

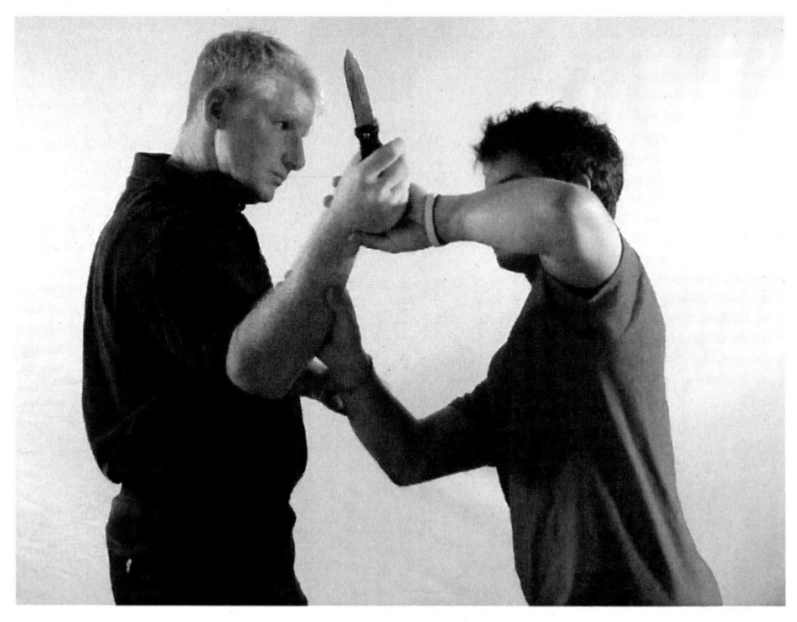

The primary objective in defense against an armed attacker is to control the weapon.

he drops to the ground, and the student delivers a knee into his head while still maintaining control of the weapon. It is only at this point that we have the student disarm the weapon, which often has already fallen from the attacker's grasp.

We teach our students to fight with everything they've got (knees, feet, teeth, and anything else available to attack any part of his body they can) while maintaining a grip on the weapon. If their grip should come loose, the number-one rule is to regain control of the weapon (if running still isn't an option). Of course, the overriding goal is always to escape as soon as possible. Once they have escaped, they are taught to get help immediately and report the incident to the authorities.

Martial artists often balk at the incredible simplicity of these tactics. Yet everyone who has ever taken our course instantly agrees that simple is better. I have taught more than 100 such courses, and in virtually every case where we attackers were able to shoot or stab or strike the defender, it was because he or she tried something fancy or lost control of the weapon.

Keep it smart, simple, and spirited, and you have a really great chance of surviving and even taking these dangerous criminals out of circulation!

SURVIVING ATTACKS BY MULTIPLE ASSAILANTS

Dealing with a gang that is intent on harming you is a very scary and dangerous proposition. Again, the fear and adrenal paralysis are very difficult to overcome. Yet if they are not overcome, the consequences can be lethal. Fortunately, most gang attacks are committed by unskilled amateurs who use the gang mentality to conquer their own feelings of weakness and powerlessness.

Nevertheless, I recommend never assuming that any gang is anything less than dangerous. Very sophisticated, well-trained gangs exist that are adept at setting victims up for a really bad hit. If you do find yourself in a meeting with such a group, you had better act fast and well, or it could be the end of your road.

Either way, there are tactics that can work quite well to help you survive and escape a gang attack. (Notice I said escape, not go chop-sockey and kick ass against an army of big bad guys like Neo in the movie *The Matrix*.) Once again, the trick is to not succumb to the strong fear and paralysis that flood your mind and body in such an extremely stressful type of encounter. I experienced intense fear in each of my gang attacks. This fear often produced that nasty paralysis where nothing at all seems to work. Even so, I still survived relatively unscathed because my tormentors were not adept fighters. Had I possessed the ability to stay sharp and present mentally (which training such as FAST Defense has proven to impart), I could have dealt with each attack much more skillfully.

The absolute worst thing a victim can do is to allow the gang to swarm in and take away any avenue of escape. Typically, the victim gets locked into tunnel vision, losing the peripheral vision that would facilitate moving and getting out of the center of the mess. In FAST training, we use the concept of "stacking" as a means to avoid getting surrounded by a gang. The coach's voice breaks the student's tunnel vision with the command of, "Stack them up!" This verbal cue breaks the spell of paralysis by triggering the low brain into action and prompting the student to quickly assess the situation and take the best avenue to either escape or fight. We run each student through a short series of interactive scenarios where the intensity is raised slightly each time the student's ability to deal with the adrenal fear rush builds.

In just a few hours we can get students who have been conditioned to freeze up entirely in past situations to take action and fight like demons possessed. For prior multiple-assault victims who are still traumatized, this can be life changing.

* * *

These are just some of the applications of the powerful adrenal stress response training technology. The potential for other applications is limited only by the imagination. Virtually any vocation that requires people to work under stressful situations can be greatly enhanced by these methods.

Chapter 12

Debunking Some Common Self-Defense Myths

In my line of work, I come across a stunning array of myths and beliefs surrounding every facet of self-defense. These range from ordinary commonsense questions to outlandish and even bizarre ideas about what happens in real-life encounters. Addressing these myths and misconceptions is paramount in teaching self-defense because they often dictate action (or inaction) that is ineffective at best and dangerous at worst. In the worst-case scenario, these ideas can get people killed. The beauty of adrenal stress response training is that it provides a laboratory where these various theories can be field-tested in as realistic an environment as possible. It is also invaluable in its ability to debunk the myths because it provides tangible evidence of their fallacy.

MYTH #1: STREET FIGHTS LAST A LONG TIME

As I sit here writing, an old issue of *Black Belt* magazine sits on my desk. Known and respected for objectively covering the world of martial arts, *Black Belt* diligently reports on a wide range of styles and subjects. One of the articles is on a two-day, real-life self-defense "Battle School."

One line in particular catches my eye: "The average street fight lasts an average of three minutes, so students must develop their cardio-respiratory and muscular endurance." In truth, physical conditioning and even physical strength, although helpful, are not the primary factors in the ability to defend oneself. I also have to question the accuracy of the statement that the average street fight lasts three minutes. Having been in dozens of real fights and witnessed many more, I recall only one that lasted anywhere near three minutes. That was the time mentioned earlier, when a fellow recon marine and I were ambushed by a group of five or six "fellow" marines from another unit on our military base in Hawaii. The ensuing fight lasted maybe two minutes (though it seemed like hours), and believe it or not, no one was hurt very badly.

Based on my experience, this altercation was ridiculously long. Virtually all of my other fights were over after the first few blows were thrown. Real fights simply do not go on for very long before one person is hurt or loses heart and gives up. Long fights typically exist only in the movies or the ring, not the real world.

I have had more than 35,000 fights in the bulletman suit. The suit allows me to cheat like crazy and take multiple shots that are harder than ones I have successfully used in real fights, and yet in the suit I keep on fighting. In FAST Defense we want our students to go into oxygen debt so they can experience how adrenaline keeps the body going when the mind is screaming to quit. A brutally long fight where we fight back hard and sustain up to a dozen solid knockout blows can last as long as 30 seconds. By the end, the student and bulletman both collapse in absolute exhaustion (although we still make our students get up and move to safety).

I'm not actually certain of how long the gang fight in Hawaii lasted because the adrenal fear rush distorts any sense of time. It could have been only one minute, or it could have been as long as three. The truth is I really don't know. And neither do most people who get into fights. The part of the brain that continues to function under duress is not capable of determining time. Therefore, I would submit that many fighters and victims think their fights went much longer than they actually did. When we show our students the videos of their fights against the bulletmen, without fail they note that the fight seemed much longer than it actually was on the video.

When a fight does go long, lack of skill is typically a factor. The marines who attacked my buddy and me had enough time to kill us if they'd had any fighting sense. Although he and I were both trained martial artists and special forces marines, we had never taken any formal adrenal stress response training. We did the most common thing—freeze and flail. Although I finally managed to break through the paralysis toward the end, the fact remains that if a fight goes on for very long, it is almost always because the people in it are not connecting good, solid blows.

Real fights between skilled combatants are wild and crazy, and people get hurt. Typically, one or two good shots take the fight out of someone. And typically it's the person who gets the first good strike in who prevails. But because of the propensity to freeze or flail under duress, many combatants never get a good shot in, other than lucky haymakers or the like.

FAST Defense physical training is really very simple. We teach people how to break the freeze effects of adrenaline and fear by focusing all that power into simple strikes to vulnerable areas on an attacker. When a person knows how to fight with total commitment and focus, chances are the fight will be over very quickly, typically in 20 seconds or less.

MYTH #2: FIGHTING BACK WILL GET YOU KILLED

I am surprised and saddened that various self-defense instructors and other "experts" in the field are still perpetrating this myth. Yet all too often I hear of new cases where people—primarily women—have received such an admonition. Probably well-intentioned but horribly misguided, this advice can be disastrous.

Although law enforcement agencies have taken the "don't fight back" stance in the past, they have done a complete reversal in recent years. Most self-defense experts now overwhelmingly favor fighting back in most cases. So why is submission still so often prescribed and presented as the safest alternative?

My theory is that a combination of inadequate training, poor socialization, and "good ol' boy" mentality historically conditioned women to play the consummate victim and simply submit without a fight ("be nice," "don't make a scene"). With all this working against them, women typically were not empowered to fight back. Thus there were most likely many incidents where women made half-hearted, frail attempts to resist, which may indeed have resulted in attacks of greater severity in some cases, leading law enforcement agencies to take the "no fight" stance.

Then there is what I refer to as the "good ol' boy" network, which is invested in preventing women from being strong and empowered. Although things are slowly changing, this network is still alive and well. In every profession, from law enforcement to politics to business to education, this fear-based mentality continues to exist and perpetuate the victimization of women. Recently I heard of a high school gym teacher who pointedly told female students to just "relax" and "take it" if attacked. His advice was that they should carry condoms to have their attacker "cooperatively" wear while raping them. Incidentally, this pearl of wisdom was imparted in the presence of the boys in the class.

The bottom line is that even when defenders lack any practical self-defense training and all of the odds would appear to be against them, fighting back is more often successful than not. Remember, the vast majority of attackers are frightened, disempowered individuals seeking a sense of control or power in their own lives by victimizing others. They prey on the weak and frail and do not want or expect a fight. When the chosen "victim" does not respond accordingly, most assailants will back off. Among those who have benefited from the technology of adrenal stress response training, such success stories abound.

Are there times when a victim should choose not to fight back? On rare occasions, yes. At times a victim may believe that he or she has a better chance of surviving by acquiescing than by resisting. Such a case might be an armed gang robbery or rape, where the odds of successful defense are almost impossible. Or perhaps when the victim is making a conscious choice in an attempt to save a child or another loved one. But the operative word is "choice." The person should *choose* to submit or *choose* to fight back, but the choice should be an informed and conscious one, not a fear-based response. No matter what the end result, FAST Defense arms people with many new choices and the power to act on those choices. And even if people choose to cooperate with an attacker, their mental and emotional states are better after the fact than if they were simply victims who felt they had no options. When someone makes a conscious choice to either submit or resist, that person is operating from a place of power.

MYTH #3: THE GROIN IS A "BAD" TARGET

It feels silly to even write about this, but it is another myth that is still perpetuated in various ways by various sources.

Recall the police officer mentioned earlier who trains SWAT teams in self-defense by hard sparring in the conventional martial arts manner. Whenever discussing the groin as a target, this police officer is emphatic about his inability to deliver a strike to the groin in his training sessions. He is convinced that the groin is a poor target because his officers were able to protect their groins very effectively while sparring.

However, sparring is quite different from real fighting. Even heavy sparring involves a degree of conscious thought and physical dexterity that is simply not available in the full adrenal rush. I have seen many skilled technical fighters stand flat on their feet and throw ineffective haymaker punches in real street encounters. Many such incidents end up in a clinch, with both fighters standing squared off, trying to get leverage over the other. To the aware fighter, it is often a simple task to throw a front kick or a knee into the groin of an opponent. Personally, I have used snap kicks to the groins of attackers in real fights with remarkable success, often causing my foe to drop like a sack of potatoes from a relatively light strike. I have also been on the receiving end of more than a few such kicks and have found the groin to be quite an effective target, sometimes much to my chagrin. Hard-core, no-holds-barred fighting contests do not allow full-contact strikes to the groin for this very reason.

Another source of this myth is the owner of a martial arts school near me in Colorado who instructs her students never to kick a man in the groin because doing so will cause him to become superhumanly strong and get you killed. Her reasoning is based on the personal accounts of women who were not adequately trained and made half-hearted kicks to the groins of their attackers. The guys became incensed and fought even harder. I am sure there are cases where people who were inadequately trained to deal with the effects of the adrenaline rush have had this experience. But my own experience and that of my students is that the groin is an excellent target, particularly when the defender strikes with the power and focus that FAST Defense training produces.

A third source of this myth that I'm aware of is a friend who grew up in New York City. He feels the stigma of growing up in "the city" is that he's supposed to be rough and tough. The stories of his exploits are elaborate and (in my book) unrealistic tales of flying spin kicks and other highly technical techniques that he's supposedly used in real fights. I have always taken his accounts with a grain of salt, but the clincher came one evening when I mentioned having used groin kicks in real fights and he was visibly offended. This was apparently outside his code of ethical fighting, and he said as much. I remember being amazed by this coming from someone who was supposedly such a fighter. (Inner-city survival would be pretty rough under such a code!) My sense is that he learned much more about street fighting from watching movies and hearing the many embellished stories than actual fighting on the streets.

As with most myths, each of these three arguments is based on at least a glimmer of reason. Yet each fails to measure up under scrutiny. The law enforcement officer rightly found that the groin is not a good target in martial arts sparring, where the combatant is psychologically prepared and is somewhat expecting the strike. A typical sparring stance slants the lower body so that the groin is not a readily available target. Yet in real-life combat, many fighters adopt a squared-off stance where the groin is an inviting and effective target.

The argument that a groin strike against a male will make him really pissed off and empower him with superhuman strength probably stems from the actual experience of women who failed to strike with focus and power because they were not trained to deal with the effects of the adrenal stress rush. Yet based on my own experience and that of my former students, a good, swift knee kick or even slap to the groin is usually enough to stop a fight in its tracks. At the very least, it slows down the attacker enough for you to make the next strike, and the next as necessary.

Finally, while there may have been certain codes of ethics in some parts of the world in the days of old, those ethics are all but irrelevant in all but the most innocent environments today. In the small town in New England where I grew up, there were unspoken rules about not kicking our schoolmates in the groin, and we surely didn't use any weapons or gang up against each other. Today, gang attacks and weapons attacks are commonplace. Suffice it to say that a simple kick to the groin is well within the "moral" limits of defending against almost anyone who might be attacking you.

My stance is that there is no such thing as a "bad" target if the defender strikes with conviction and power. Some targets may be better than others. But when it comes to the male groin, no manner of conditioning or weight training can make this area impervious to strikes while under duress. (Although some guys have tried!)

MYTH #4: A SMALLER, WEAKER PERSON HAS NO CHANCE AGAINST A LARGER, STRONGER ATTACKER

Obviously, fighting back against a large and determined attacker will most often be harder than fighting a smaller one, but when you consider the reality that most attackers are looking for an easy victim and not a fight, the determined defender's odds substantially improve no matter what the size of the assailant. Another factor is that big guys have often learned to use their size as intimidation, and because they have never felt the need to learn to fight, many of these behemoths fold when their bluff is called. I have faced such monsters in my bulletman armor more times than I can recall, and ironically, many did not hit as hard as I'd expected.

There is also the empirical evidence that "attitude" is the preeminent factor in determining whether someone survives an attack. In other words, the person who can crank up and focus the adrenaline fear rush in his or her defense is usually the victor. Fancy technical training is not as helpful as the ability to fight for all you are worth!

You'll recall the earlier discussion of research involving convicted felons, which reveal that, almost without exception, these predators looked for easy prey that communicated victim mentality before perpetrating their assaults. Physical size itself was not as much a factor in their choice of victims as were the other cues of body language, eye contact, awareness of environment, and so on. Their potential victims could be large or small, as long as they passed the initial screening process. Thus, even a very small person who can communicate assertiveness through correct body language will usually thwart an attack before it begins. And even if that small person does draw an attacker, good verbal skills and eye contact typically work to diffuse the situation. If all else fails and an attack does occur, I can vouch firsthand for the power and spirit that physically small women, men, and even children can assert. It is these very people who usually ring my bell with surprising power against my bulletman suit, simply because smaller physical size is so unassuming. When such a person taps into the emotional/biochemical adrenal rush and applies it in a full-force strike, the power is truly amazing. Even with 35 pounds of the finest body armor available, the force is discernible. An attacker who is not looking for a fight will probably back off immediately. If not, then he'd better be ready to take that face full of claw that a FAST Defense-trained person can and will dish out. As the old adage says, "It's not the size of the dog in the fight, but the size of the fight in the dog."

Obviously, physical conditioning helps. But I have seen many a pencil-pushing, out-of-shape office worker use adrenaline to crank up and knock bigger, stronger opponents silly. I have seen short, timid women go mama bear on guys twice their weight and size. I have seen the proverbial skinny weakling go medieval on a big, macho good ol' boy and knock him out cold. When it comes to prevailing in a fight, the ability to use the emotional and biochemical effects of stress and fear as power far override physical strength and size or lack thereof.

These days many people are looking for a magic pill that will render them invincible against any threat. No such magic cure exists, but FAST Defense does teach the real-life skills needed to handle most threatening situations very effectively in a very short time.

MYTH #5: A GOOD SELF-DEFENSE COURSE MUST TEACH BLOCKING SKILLS

A while back I was discussing various facets of self-defense with someone who is also considered an "expert" in the self-defense field. We were pretty well aligned in our beliefs and philosophies until he made the comment that every self-defense course must include blocking skills. This is a rather common misconception that is a result of thinking in the traditional technique-based paradigm versus a concept-based one.

Although I believe there are cases where a block of sorts might be useful, I also believe that focusing on executing a block in a real-life encounter can lead to serious problems. I should qualify this. Long ago I had an experience where a guy tried to take my head off with a baseball bat in a place called Luneta Park in Manila. Fortunately, I turned in time (cued by my buddy's jaw dropping as he saw the attacker come up behind me) and was able to get my hands up to protect my head in time to save myself some serious brain damage. In truth, it really wasn't a block at all as much as simply getting my hands up in what I now know as the red alert defensive stance. I was immersed in the Filipino arts at the time and was actually able to disarm the guy of the bat. This occurred years before I created FAST Defense or the red alert stance, so the movement was instinctual.

I have never seen or applied a formal martial arts block in a real altercation. Think about it. If you are trying to employ any technical block at all, then you are allowing the other person to dictate the fight. The adage "The best defense is a good offense" definitely applies here. Our students have shown time and again the ability to strike preemptively in our courses. I am constantly impressed and amazed from inside the bulletman suit at how quickly our training methods teach someone to slam home that first strike, even when we know exactly what he or she is going to throw! Once that first strike hits the mark, we bulletmen quickly lose control as the students overwhelm us in their adrenalized fury. Even though we're cheating like crazy by not responding to various strikes at all, in actuality that first shot pretty much takes us out of the fight.

I should add that in the suit we do try to get strikes in on the students, both initially and during the fights. Typically the students are so adrenalized that they barely realize they have been struck at all. Proper combat mind-set is probably the single most important factor in how people fare in an altercation. Those who can flip the switch and totally go for it almost always prevail. Stopping to think in order to block typically puts you into a defensive mind-set, breaks the focus necessary to flip that switch, and gives the attacker the advantage, often with disastrous results.

So in anticipation of the skeptic's question, "Do we just let them hit us with our guard down?" I say emphatically, "No!" Having the hands up in good protective guard, where the hands are at least eye level and the elbows are angled in to protect centerline, is protection enough. This protective position in unison with a preemptive strike offers all that is needed in one swift movement. My buddy Peyton Quinn and I did some interesting tests for a video for NAPMA. In it we tried various strikes against a defender with our arms in this protective position. We were astounded when, as the attacker, we both found it very difficult to get through the defense to land a strike. Most attackers throw wild roundhouse punches that are really very easy to avoid for the person trained in watching the many cues that warn of an impending attack. Combining this protective position with a ferocious attack to vulnerable areas on the attacker quickly enables anyone to gain control of the fight, regardless of physical size or strength. The one who controls the fight wins.

FAST Defense instructors continually remind students to keep their hands up and elbows in. It is very important to make sure the defender's hands are high enough to protect against a roundhouse or overhand punch. The propensity to drop the hands occurs most often with passive students, so instructors are gentle, firm, and consistent in retraining them to maintain the protective guard. Combined with the myriad other skills taught in FAST Defense, this ensures a very high success rate in students who later end up being attacked.

MYTH #6: DISARMING ARMED ATTACKERS IS A GOOD IDEA

I have been fortunate to train with some incredibly talented people in some very fun and challenging martial arts styles. Many of these include various techniques for disarming attackers wielding guns, knives, and sticks. Although I enjoy playing with these often-elaborate techniques, I would not try to use them against a real-life armed assailant. I have been cut with a knife in a real attack and have survived an armed attack. Even with a pretty good amount of martial training behind me, the thought of disarming my attackers never even entered my mind in either situation. The fear that occurs during an armed attack is so intense that my mind simply blanked out in the madness of the moment. This is not to say that some people haven't pulled off disarms in real attacks. I know a guy who actually used a movie-style reverse crescent kick to knock a knife out of another guy's hand in a street fight. And I watched a friend of mine have a pair of nunchakus kicked out of his hand by a roundhouse kick during a ridiculous drunken brawl. I also know of an elderly Southern grandmother who walked right up to her gun-wielding burglar, yanked the piece right out of his hand, and scolded him for threatening her! Although a disarm can be pulled off, I strongly caution against trying such a move in most cases.

Unless you have ever experienced it, you cannot imagine the intense fear a weapon-wielding attacker can provoke. Almost instantly, the adrenal fear rush drastically limits fine motor control and rational thinking by cutting the victim off from the part of the brain that houses complex techniques like weapon disarms.

Additionally, most assaults with weapons are used for intimidation to get a victim to comply with the attacker's wishes. If it is a crime of possession like a burglary, the best tactic is to give up that possession. Someone who is thinking of performing a disarm (and usually not rationally) might easily miss a crucial chance to end the confrontation before it ever becomes physical. Worse yet, an inept attempt at a disarm could prove disastrous by incensing the attacker into using the weapon against you. A high percentage of police officers who have been shot were shot with their own sidearm after the perpetrator took it away from them. Each of these incidents started with the weapon under the officer's control, and yet the gun was used against the officer. The situation is even more dangerous when the weapon is under the bad guy's control to start with.

However, if the attacker is intent on taking you to a secondary location or harming you right where you are, the best chance you have is get both hands on the weapon and weapon hand, and kick, knee, bite, head butt, and do everything you can to hurt him. Only after he is good and "softened up" should you even begin to think about getting the weapon away from him. Keeping it simple is the safest way to go and the very best way to live through the attack—and hopefully even get the attacker incarcerated.

MYTH #7: MEN DON'T NEED SELF-DEFENSE

This is another myth that seems ludicrous, yet I find it is still a very commonly held belief everywhere I go. Many FAST Defense courses are filled with women who see the need for self-defense as a result of incidents that either they or someone they know have experienced. But mysteriously, men are much less likely to attend these readily available courses.

Self-defense courses originally arose as a way to help women who were prey to the bad guys of the world but were not willing or able to engage in the rigors of traditional, old-school martial arts training. These courses were typically taught by martial artists or law enforcement professionals and targeted almost exclusively to women; "real men" joined the local karate school to hone their self-defense skills. It is my experience that many guys feel taking a self-defense course is an admission of weakness. They tend to believe that by virtue of being men they are somehow supposed to know how to take care of themselves. Yet men flock to martial arts schools that will supposedly teach them all about self-defense (and typically fall well short of the goal). Why is this? It seems that martial arts practice—engaging in combatives through complex physical movements that test dexterity and prowess—is a more socially acceptable activity for men. And it may be that the journey to the esteemed black belt allures men to the martial arts in our goal-driven society.

Though increased violence in our society is clearly dictating a greater need for self-defense training for both genders than ever before, men still hold on to the conditioning that keeps them from entering self-defense classes. Yet men are accosted as much as women are. It just happens in a different way. From early childhood to adulthood, men experience a barrage of challenges and threats from macho jerks who challenge their masculinity, sexual prowess, and so on. Sadly, no one ever teaches them how to deal effectively and realistically with these threats.

It was with this in mind that I created the first organization to offer adrenal stress response self-defense training exclusively for men back in 1990. Although it was in the time of the men's movement, my motivation was not to capitalize on the sensitive new-age guys of the world. It actually started with my friends and fellow bulletmen, who simply wanted to enjoy the rewards of this powerful training that we were providing to women. After all, most of us had joined the martial arts because of some sort of previous bad experience or victimization. So I started marketing adrenal stress response training to men in Boulder. The men who were drawn to the course were a rare breed of very cool guys. Typically they were in the 30-plus age group. Also typical was the common bond of having experienced some sort of verbal or physical attack. All of them had some previous experience that pushed them over the denial threshold into admitting that they were not supermen capable of handling every adversity. Men are verbally and physically assaulted in many different ways in our society, and worse yet, they are taught that the natural feelings of fear and vulnerability that result are failings rooted in their inadequacy.

The bottom line is that men need self-defense just as much as women do. But it takes strength and maturity for men to admit that they are not invulnerable. For our male graduates, this admission of vulnerability becomes their greatest strength as they learn to use their fear and emotions as a tremendous source of power. These men leave the course stronger of heart and much more capable of handling future macho altercations.

MYTH #8: MEN AND WOMEN SHOULD BE TAUGHT EXACTLY THE SAME WAY IN MARTIAL ARTS

The martial arts world has evolved a great deal over the years, particularly in the past decade or so. The "old school" mentality from back when classes were often taught in garages or backyards and women and children were typically not invited has, for the most part, been overtaken by the new wave of successful martial arts schools where both children and women are taking a much more involved role.

In addition, the role of women as instructors and as students has also become quite significant. In the old days women had a very rough time dealing with the good ol' boy mentality prevalent in the martial arts community. Some of these women persevered, with huge credit due them for doing so. Others left those schools to start their own, where they wouldn't have to deal with such unnecessary abuse. And sadly, many of these early female students left the martial arts altogether because they never found the desired feeling of safety that led them to explore the martial arts in the first place. Over the years many men have become more sensitive to the unique issues that can arise for women in the martial arts environment.

In my travels teaching FAST Defense at martial arts schools across America and abroad, I have the opportunity to meet many female martial arts instructors and to hear firsthand what they have and in some cases still must go through in this highly competitive industry. Although most of the good ol' boy mentality is gone, there are still complicated dynamics between the genders in the martial arts world, even in the best-case scenario.

An incident that occurred early in my teaching career illustrates the unique challenges that many male school owners and female students face in a traditional martial arts environment. The experience taught me a great deal, though it came at a cost. It is my hope that the story will help others prevent such occurrences at their schools.

It started as a typical Wednesday open sparring night. The standard eight to ten regulars were there, as well as a couple of guys from another local school who often showed up to play. Most of the participants were men, but there were a couple of women as well. One woman was Terri, an established black belt, and the other was Kathy, a blue belt, who was outwardly pretty tense but showed a lot of heart. I always sensed there was something going on inside that she was trying to cover up but felt it wasn't my place to dig where I didn't belong. Heck, I was a martial artist, not a therapist, and none of my previous instructors had ever asked how I was "feeling"—you either showed up for sparring or you didn't.

The group paired off and followed the standard rules of agreement on the level of intensity before squaring off. I was absorbed in working with a young guy who was preparing for an upcoming test when I detected a change in the group's energy. I turned to see Kathy, the blue belt, quickly bow off the floor. She had been paired up with Jim, one of those guys who by nature goes harder than he likes to admit. He stood there with shoulders shrugged in a confused gesture and voiced that he had accidentally popped Kathy "lightly" and she "just ran off." Throwing him an irritated "we've discussed this problem before" kind of glance, I left the floor to check on Kathy. Terri, the black belt, was already there consoling her. It looked like Kathy might be crying, but she refused to show me any tears. Putting up a stiff upper lip, she stated she was "fine" and that everything was okay.

Terri assured me that she had the situation under control, so I returned to the floor. After I reiterated my standard warning about control and following the rules of agreement to the whole class, sparring continued. A short time later I saw Kathy leaving the school, and I went over to ask how she was doing. Again she assured me that everything was okay as she walked out the door. Terri returned to sparring and we finished the session without further incident.

A couple of weeks went by, and I saw no sign of Kathy. When I asked Terri what was up, her reply caught me off guard. Taking me aside, she explained that Kathy was in an abusive relationship and had received several beatings from her alcoholic husband over the years, one of them quite recently. This was the very reason she had originally signed up for the martial arts. My expression conveyed the incredulity common among men who simply can't comprehend why anyone would ever stay in such a relationship. Terri said it was a difficult situation and that we should give Kathy space to determine if and when she wanted to resume class. She also mentioned that being in martial arts was far different for women than it was for men. At the time I had no real concept of what she meant, nor did I have any plausible solutions.

Sadly, Kathy never returned for another class. Even worse, I later learned that she had actually tried to fight off her husband using the traditional martial arts techniques I had taught her and that her attempts at self-defense had only enraged her drunken husband into beating her worse. Needless to say, the incident hit me pretty hard, and I felt pretty helpless about it all.

This incident occurred approximately 18 years ago. I had just returned from two years of living and studying martial arts in Asia after a four-year hitch in my marine recon unit. Like most male martial arts instructors, I was a nice guy who genuinely cared about people and their ability to defend themselves. But I was way out of touch with the issues that can come up when working with women in this male-dominated environment. Now, after 17 years of teaching women's self-defense seminars with various female experts on violence against women, and having worked with literally hundreds of abuse survivors, I see the picture much more clearly.

As I see it, there are three very important issues that most martial arts schools fail to address:

1) For men, it is very difficult to understand the level of intimidation and fear that many women feel in

everyday situations that guys don't think twice about. This dynamic is definitely alive in the martial arts world. Fortunately, a lot of the good ol' boy attitude has been abandoned, though certainly not all of it. But even in progressive schools the environment can still be very challenging for women. Whether female students have any history of abuse or not, activities like sparring or grappling with the nicest of guys can trigger emotional issues. More women students leave the martial arts for these reasons than most of us realize.

2) The standard self-defense moves that were handed down to us by our instructors are often not only insufficient for dealing with the ways in which women are attacked but they can actually set up women to be more likely victims. This does not mean that the martial arts are wrong or bad but that traditional martial arts training lacks components that are critical for women to be able to deal effectively with violent confrontations. If these standard self-defense methods have gotten many a male black belt beaten by a good street fighter (and they have), imagine how many female martial artists have been hurt over the years in violent altercations.

3) The majority of attacks on women are perpetrated by someone they know. Date rape and battered woman syndrome are very real problems with very real psychological issues that require solutions far beyond the scope of physical defense techniques.

Martial arts instruction is a technique-based paradigm. Each student makes a long-term journey to learn and master the various physical techniques required of his or her respective style. The success of the new evolution of self-defense programs (EZ Defense, FAST Defense, RMCAT, and others) has shown that real-life self-defense requires more than just physical techniques.

Awareness of the following dynamics of assault and the mistakes people make under duress is crucial for self-defense to be effective:

- the socio-conditioning that can keep someone from fighting back at all
- the often debilitating effects of the adrenaline fear response
- the mind-set and intention of attackers
- the verbal skills needed to de-escalate or ward off a hostile person
- the criticality of the mind-set to fight back with absolute commitment when necessary

Simply being aware of these complicated issues goes a long way toward being more sensitive to the unique needs of female students and providing a safe environment for them to train.

MYTH #9: SELF-DEFENSE IS NOT CONSISTENT WITH A SPIRITUAL PATH

I'm based just outside of Boulder, so it's not uncommon for me to come into contact with folks who feel that taking a self-defense course unnecessarily opens the "doors to the universe" and invites potential harm and bad people into their world. In other words, some people believe that in exposing themselves to this very realistic training, they are drawing acts of violence into their lives by the law of attraction, which says that if you focus on something you will cause it to happen. Although I am a firm believer in the law of attraction, in my experience the opposite is actually true in this case. I have come to believe that such reasoning is a fear-based rationalization as opposed to a rational judgment that results from weighing all sides of the issue and consciously deciding to be truly pacifistic. This comes from denial of the realities of what humans do to each other every day. A real pacifist (which I consider myself to be) can only become so by having the choice to fight back if needed and *deciding* not to fight if that is in fact the appropriate response at the appropriate time. The person whose pacifism is not a choice but a fear-based emotional reaction is in denial. Paradoxically, such a person is more likely to give off negative, fear-based "vibes" that could actually draw a potential attacker.

What the FAST Defense process evokes is an intense desire and ability to take full responsibility for one's life. This involves breaking the fear and denial that trap many people into limited existence. Graduates of our program leave the course feeling less aggressive and more easygoing and are thus less likely to have to use their newfound skills because of the true sense of confidence they discover—confidence that predators shy away from more often than not because they are looking for the proverbial disempowered easy victim.

Having the choice to fight also gives you the choice to *not* fight if you don't want to, no matter what the reason. The key word here is *choice*!

An excellent example of this—and one of the most extraordinary people I have ever met—was Eric, a

Franciscan friar who chose to take a men's intensive course under a pseudonym because of his professional status. I greatly enjoyed some very heartfelt lunch talks before and after he took the course. He really wanted to be clear on what he would be doing in the course and why he wanted so much to take this rather extreme journey into his own dark side. Eric wanted to explore the warrior spirit that all of us have, but he felt the Catholic Church would take a very dim view of his engaging in such an extreme course. As a Franciscan friar, he felt he was expected to deny that he had a dark side. Yet he was honest enough with himself both to realize that beneath his friar exterior, his dark warrior side was alive and well and to recognize that it was a totally normal part of the human psyche.

So this kind, gentle soul showed up for the course—and unleashed a warrior the likes of which I have rarely seen. The fact that he was so in touch with his peace-loving, spiritual side allowed him to dig deep and let his darker emotions, which society says we should repress, rise to the surface and roar like a lion! I will never forget seeing his eyes shine with the blazing spirit of a gladiator as he fought for himself with all the fury of a mama bear fighting for her young.

At our final lunch together, he related that he was leaving the brotherhood. He did not believe life was meant to be lived in such a restrictive environment, and he wanted to reenter the world on his own terms. I will never forget the last words he spoke to me: "If God is love, which I truly believe to be so, then I walk out of here more filled with God than I have ever felt before. And if nothing is stronger than love, than God, then I have never been stronger than I am now." As he spoke these words, his eyes were ablaze with the spirit of life.

This man exemplified the true spirit of warriorhood. The hardest and perhaps most powerful thing we can do in life is to love ourselves enough to choose not to hurt others. This is the sign of a true warrior. The Franciscan friars lost a beautiful brother that day, but the world gained a warrior of epic proportions. His power doesn't come from big muscles, tattoos, a Mohawk haircut, or leather and chains. It comes from pure love, for himself and for mankind. This man is a true pacifist. And if he ever does have to fight, watch out.

MYTH #10: THE ADRENALINE RUSH IS A BAD THING

One question I am commonly asked after all the years of doing this work is, "Do you still get the adrenal rush?" My answer is an emphatic yes. In fact, I welcome the adrenal rush because I relish having all of that power as a source of defensive action should I need it. That doesn't mean I *will* need it, only that I will have it available should the need arise. The adrenal rush is designed to occur as a means to help us deal with stressful situations. Why deprive ourselves of millennia of human survival evolution? A few years back I began to notice that before fighting the bulletman each time, I clear my mind of any preconceived notions of specific techniques or reactions I might use. I call this "getting out of my own way" to allow the pure flow of adrenaline, spontaneous reaction, and spirit do the trick. Next I literally invite the adrenal rush to occur in my body, which feels like a warm current of electric energy coursing up my spine. The final step is to commit to explode 110 percent when necessary, particularly through a strong voice in which the adrenaline is catalyzed into physical action. Thus I have conditioned myself to bring on the adrenaline at will. Now the wary reader might ask, isn't this unrealistic, because in real situations things happen so fast there isn't time to do all this preparation. This is true. But adrenal stress response training is designed to give you a safe and controlled step-by-step methodology to condition the appropriate "go-for-it" use of adrenaline. This carries over into real-life situations where you don't have the time to consciously prepare but must react instinctively. The stories abound of students effectively dealing with very scary situations after taking this type of training.

The problem with most people is that, without proper training, this powerful biochemical and even emotional reaction can work against them. Untrained people often react disproportionately to the threat at hand, either by underreacting (passive) or by overreacting (aggressive). Remember: *If people just don't screw up in an assault, they usually come out okay.* Many victims *do* screw up. Because they have never learned how to deal with the adrenal rush, they go into a knee-jerk response that can actually get them into even worse trouble. But with proper training, adrenaline and fear can be controlled and focused appropriately and, if necessary, make you a serious force to be reckoned with. Each time someone experiences the adrenal rush in our courses, he or she learns how to work with and focus it in an appropriate manner. Even after just one FAST Defense class, students acquire an exponential gain in their ability to make a rational assessment of the threat and respond appropriately (with an assertive response) under duress. There are usually a number of potentially appropriate responses available in any situation. FAST Defense arms students with the ability to assess and react assertively and effectively.

So do I still get a good adrenal buzz? You bet I do! FAST Defense is all about using this energy as your ally. When you can trust that in a worst-case scenario you will be able to flip the switch and react, you suddenly drop all those other useless facades you used to put up to protect yourself. You can relax in the empowering knowledge that with adrenaline on your side, you have very powerful choices available to you.

Appendix

REALITY-BASED TRAINING RESOURCES

The International FAST Defense Association (IFDA) is devoted to setting up programs internationally and maintaining safety and quality control of the various organizations teaching these short but very intense self-defense seminars. Through the efforts of the IFDA and its exceptional instructors throughout North America, Europe, and Asia, this training is now accessible to more people than ever.

FAST DEFENSE

Adrenal Stress Response Training is an experiential journey and must be experienced to be fully appreciated. To find a FAST Defense training location near you, go to www.fastdefense.com and look under training locations. You may also sign up for the free *FAST Times* monthly newsletter filled with advice, tips, and more at that site.

OTHER PROGRAMS

A Woman's Epic Journey
P.O. Box 1077
Firestone, CO 80502
Web site: www.AWomansEpicJourney.com

IMPACT & Prepare
147 West 25th St., 8th Floor
New York, NY 10001-7205
Web site: www.prepareinc.com

Model Mugging
1222 Magnolia Ave. #105-202
Corona, CA 92881-2075
Web site: www.modelmugging.org

Raw Power
P.O. Box 2046
Glendale, CA 91209
Web site: www.r-a-wpower.com

Rocky Mountain Combat Applications Training (RMCAT)
Box 535
Lake George, CO 80827
Web site:www.rmcat.com.

Veterans & Families
657 Brickyard Drive
Sacramento, CA 95831
Web site: www.veteransandfamilies.org

Zen Kommando
6320 Brookside Plaza
Suite #2200
Kansas City, MO 64113